Embracing Bootstrap
LEADERSHIP

———◦ℭ◦———

*Moving from Humble Beginnings
to Christ-Centered Leadership*

WALTER AUGUST, JR.

Embracing Bootstrap Leadership

Copyright © 2014 by Walter August, Jr.

All rights reserved. No part of this book may be reproduced or transmitted in any form or by any means without written permission of the author.

ISBN: 978-0-9831132-5-6 (paperback)
        978-0-9831132-6-3 (eBook)

Published by:
True Story Press

Always in His service.
Galatians 2:20

Contents

CHAPTER ONE
Leaders Are Not Born 1

CHAPTER TWO
Good Leader, Poor Leader 13

CHAPTER THREE
Family Application. 31

CHAPTER FOUR
Having the Right Priorities. 59

CHAPTER FIVE
Speak and Think Like a Leader 81

CHAPTER SIX
Visionary Impact 91

CHAPTER SEVEN
True Friends and Prayer 103

Final Note on Leadership. 117

FOREWORD

WHAT A PRIVILEGE it is to write a foreword to Pastor Walter August's book on leadership! It was a great day when Walter became my Missions Pastor at Sugar Creek Baptist Church. He displayed outstanding leadership and expanded the mission work dramatically. We helped plant over sixty new churches in the Houston area and beyond. Together, we made inroads into new countries and established partnerships with the indigenous leadership wherever we traveled.

Walter's leadership style is simple and easy to apply. God directs him to see a need, an empty place that must be filled, and he moves forward by God's provision to fill it. At Bethel's Family Church, he began in an apartment building and then moved into a small shopping center. From there, he moved to a school auditorium and then purchased a failing church building. Today, at that location, there is a thriving church

FOREWORD

with a multitude of ministries that are changing lives daily.

That Walter calls me his "father in the ministry" is very humbling, and I am grateful for any influence that I might have had on his ministry. But he has gone far beyond anything I have ever attempted. Walter has not let anything stop him from moving forward. He has the gift of faith and leadership and truly lives like nothing is impossible with God.

Pastor Fenton Moorhead

CHAPTER ONE

Leaders Are Not Born

MY HUMBLE BEGINNINGS go back to Abbeville, Louisiana. I was born fifth of a total of nine kids, sharing a room, raised in the Rural South, with family struggles and parents who lacked education. As children, my siblings and I saw our peers and the things that they had, from clothing to toys. They got store-bought toys, but we had to make ours. But out of that humble beginning, we always knew we had substance. We had quality and not just a quantity of things. We had what we really needed versus what we saw and thought we wanted.

I really didn't know how poor I was until I ventured out from my own common surroundings. I would go across town, less than a half a mile away from my cousin's house, and I knew there was a difference. Even as a child, you see those different things.

However, the more I think about it, it was a sweet form of God's hand keeping us in a very humble state because it ties into the scriptures. Christ asks that his followers walk in the spirit of submission and humility. If anyone wants to be great, he will be a servant to all (MARK 10:42-45). Even when it comes down to leadership, leaders must walk the same way. So out of that spirit of humble beginnings you get more realization of how powerful God is, when you walk humbly with him.

Despite family issues and the struggles of growing up, knowing that all of your needs were met, *now* you can appreciate things you *didn't* have.

One-Person Movement

All through history, a great move of God always starts with one person—all through *His* history. Matter of fact, in Genesis, Chapter 12, God tells Abraham,

> "Get from amongst your kinfolks. Take your wife Sarah. Take your family." And he tells Abraham, "Go to a land I will show you. And those who bless you, I will bless them. And those who curse you, I will curse them. And I will make you the father of many nations."

God planted that in Abraham's soul and Abraham took off. When people pray, in many cases, somewhere in their prayer, they say, "the God of Abraham, Isaac, and Jacob." Abraham's son, Isaac; Isaac's son Jacob, turned into Israel—the twelve tribes of Israel; it falls on Joseph, and goes into the lineage of David, and then comes to Christ on the other end. So you see, great things are started with one person. And Christ changed not only his community, but also the whole world.

> "For God so loved the world that he gave his only begotten *Son,*" one person, that the world should live (JOHN 3:16).

You can go back to Noah and his family. The human race was saved, based on the righteousness of Noah. All through the Bible, the *one-person movement* is woven. Also, Esther saves a whole race of people, because she marries the king. She speaks to the King. He gives her the desires of her heart, that Israel, the Jews, are saved and spared because it was for such a time as this that Esther rose.

Think of the Montgomery Boycott in Alabama—Rosa Parks decided, "Listen, I'm not standing up." It wasn't Dr. King that started the movement. It was the spirit in Parks to not get up. And had she gotten up, there's a probability that we never would have heard about Dr. Martin Luther King at the level that God used him. And the *one-person movement* is still happening today. But God has always and will continue to work through that one person. Isaiah had it right when he said, "Lord, listen. Send me. Send me. Let me be the one to go (ISAIAH 6:8)."

Handicapped and Victorious

When we get to that point where we say, "Lord, send me," the devil can discourage us so much. Sometimes it's our past. Sometimes it's our inability to believe that God has called us, because nothing has worked out in our lives before. If the truth were known, all of us are saddled with some kind of *handicap*, something that trips us up, cramps our style, gets in our way. Consider what Paul says in 2nd Corinthians:

> "To keep me from becoming conceited because of these surpassingly great revelations, there was given me a thorn in my flesh, a messenger of Satan, to torment me. Three times I pleaded with the Lord to take it away from me." But he said to me, "My grace is sufficient for you, for my power is made perfect in weakness." Therefore I will boast all the more gladly about my weaknesses, so that Christ's power may rest on me. That is why, for Christ's sake, I delight in weaknesses, in insults, in hardships, in persecution, in difficulties. For when I am weak, then I am strong" (2 Cor. 12:7-10).

We do not fully know what handicap the Apostle Paul had. Some believe it was a defect in speech. Others say it was malaria fever, due to his long travels. Still others say it was poor eyesight. But Paul learned to be fruitful and to live well with his problems, whatever they were. In fact, he made it pay rich, spiritual dividends. Just hear him say that he gloried in his infirmity, that the power of Christ may be released through him. He seems to say, "If I cannot be rid of it, then I will accept it, dedicate it, and glorify my heavenly Father with it." He *uses* his handicap to gain power from God for God.

Claiming Victory

If it's not a physical handicap, lameness of some sort, a prolonged illness, then it is likely to be something psychological, some kink in the mind, perhaps, that makes us say and do things we later regret. My sister, for example, dealing with foolish men, found herself having to run the gamut of psychological issues in more ways than one.

I used to envy guys at school that had the big afro. They had all the girls around them and the whole nine yards. But, most of those kids who seemingly had everything are not any good right now. One guy that I grew up with was a great artist. He could draw anything. He went into the military, came back, got out in the world, and ended up on drugs. His whole life, ruined. In my hometown, drugs became a means for eradication of many young men, gifted individuals, and young girls.

Even when marijuana became prevalent, people were passing the joint around, but I just could not wrap my head around it. My mindset was, "If I have a dollar I have to buy some food." I couldn't puff on a cigarette and watch my money go away in a billow of smoke. I couldn't relate to that. I thought, "That's wasted money. Are you out of your mind?" So I didn't get involved with that.

The greatest obstacle of being handicapped — or challenged or disabled or whatever label we will be using this year — is not the condition but the stigma society associates with it. But in my life, the very things that were popular with trends and keeping in style, based on our beginnings never phased me and my siblings. There was no thought that we *had to* do this or wear that because we couldn't have it. Not having things was a blessing for us. The results of having those things messed up so many people that I knew. Instead, we received substance.

The truth is, we are valuable because of who we are, not because of how we look or what we accomplish. And that applies to all of us, the disabled and the temporarily able-bodied alike. When our "thorns," infirmities and handicaps, threaten to discourage us, we can remember great souls like Paul of Tarsus, and a multitude of others, both great and small: your Mom and Dad; grandparents and great grandparents. I thank God for my handicaps, for through them I have found myself, my work, and my God. Let us glory in our infirmities that the Power of Christ may be revealed in us. God will help us to win that victory.

An Important Question

Before we progress too far, I must address an important question. Someone may ask, "Why should I lead?" Part of understanding leadership, and understanding life itself, is the knowledge that you didn't make it on your own. I didn't make it on my own, so what would give me some sense of entitlement that it has to be about me? It has to be about something greater than you.

God, in His infinite wisdom, has gifted us and designed us, just as He wanted to, for his Divine Purpose that we might be a light; we might be a vessel; we might be an instrument in *His hands* to be a life-changer, one that brings about stabilization in people's lives. We want to be used by God. That's the "*instrument mind-set*" that we all should have. So my answer to the question, why one should lead, points to two things we must remember: 1) we are terminal, and 2) we owe a debt.

1. We Are Terminal

So often, the challenge for a lot of us is the question, "Do I have it to give?" We are afraid of giving our last. We are afraid that somebody will pass us up financially. But consider this:

On a trip back from Kenya, I had altitude sickness and whatever else the travel medication was doing to us. My wife, Ruby, and I were both feeling the same—head spinning; stomach churning. I looked at her and said, "I have money in my wallet. I have a home. We have vehicles in our garage. And you know something? When you're sick, none of that stuff matters."

Part of the common denominator for all men and women, is to remember: *we are terminal*. Most people don't calculate, in their living, that they are dying. Well, I am a realist. Because of that, I want to make sure that we sow; that we give; that our life is a continuation, in spirit, of what we sowed in the physical. It will only be evident by what we actually sow with our own hands. Some people can make it about money, but it's really about your life. If you *sow your life*, then everything else will go along with it. Because you can sow money and still not have your life attached to it. And that's just making a donation, but that is not what Christ has given to us. God gave His life that we might live. It has to be about something greater than you.

2. We Owe A Debt

You need to remember that God in His infinite wisdom reminds Israel constantly, in Deuteronomy, "Do not forget... Do not forget (6:12 & 8:11,14)." So I say to you, "Do not forget where the Lord has bought you from." You were bought at a price. He got you out of captivity. The greatest danger to any man, any woman, boy, or girl is when God has done tremendous good to you, and you forget God. He is the sustainer and the blesser of all good things in your life. "All good things come from the father of lights (JAMES 1:17)." You never want to forget from whence you have come. Never. And I can underscore that all day long. Never forget where you came from.

A cautionary tale was illustrated in a movie, called "Imitation of Life," that came out in the 1930s. It's about a fair-skinned Black woman, Peola, who had a dark-skinned mother, Delilah. But Peola didn't want to identify with her mother. There is a scene in the movie where Peola is working in a little boutique somewhere and she was passing herself off as White. Well, her mother was looking for her and didn't know where she was. But her mother showed up at the boutique. Delilah went in, and said, "Daughter, how are you doing?" But Anglos were in the store at the time, so Peola replied, "Ma'am, who are you?" And she broke her mother's heart. I think the breaking of her mother's heart caused her mother to get sick. So, Delilah died. At the funeral, Peola was walking behind the casket crying and boo-hooing. But her mother was gone. The danger of forgetting, and it happens far too often with too many good leaders, is that it comes back to haunt you.

You have to have a mind-frame that you owe a debt. Not only should you *not* forget, but remember you've been put on this earth so that the world in which you live is better because you are here. You have to make up your mind to leave it better than you found it. You can't leave it the same, because it never stays the same. Either you take from it or you add to it.

When you are born into this land, one of the first things you do is suck up somebody's oxygen, and as long as you are here, you keep sucking up oxygen. Well, if you keep breathing, what are the benefits for you sucking up all this oxygen? It has to produce something! To take and not give is one of the greatest sins of humanity and leaders, in particular.

You have to always give more than you take. That's the struggle with our nation and our world. How much money do you truly need to live on? If you had five million dollars in the bank, would that be enough to retire, do some wonderful things, and bless some other people? Surely, it would be enough. Unfortunately, the caption of *Greed* has set in so strongly that money is all over the place, but leadership is no where to be found. I'm talking about *godly* leadership—leadership that makes a difference for generations to come. The money is there. Leadership is what's lacking.

Life Letters

I first met Pastor August when I was going on my first Mission trip to Africa (Kenya), and he taught me that going on mission is what we are called to do. Once you go on mission, you will never be the same, but you got to have the heart to Love, Serve and Give. You will actually see God at work. My eyes has truly been open. I have learned how to love with compassion. I learned how to put everything aside and go do what God said what we must do. You've got to put all your trust in God and allow Him to lead you. So when I hear the phrase "Leaders are not Born," it simply tells me that there is a lot of work to be done and you have to show that you are not afraid to work, lead from the front and not from the rear. It's a lot more than just preaching 52 Sunday's in a year. You have six more days in those weeks that require more work.

REVEREND OTIS CAREY

Great leaders are not born; they are molded from the same fabric of life granted each of us, but the etching on their life forms just the right depth for the passage of greatness to flow through them. What cripples many, has strengthened Walter August, Jr. What leaves horrid scar tissue and mangled minds for most, has only distinguished him from the crowd. What saps the strength from the majority of us and leaves us too weakened to reach greatness, swaddles him like a healing balm and heightens his determination.

Great leaders are not born, but can be made from devastating patterns of abuse. By a sheer desire to end the curse of generations of torn-apart families in his history and by the healing love of God, he has learned to celebrate and model what a healthy marriage should look like.

Great leaders are not born; they are kneaded from the raw clay of humanity and prepared by the fires of life. Life's kiln has burned hotter in Walter August, Jr.'s life then many, but it has made him stronger and more resilient. Those who follow him are better for their journey. We recognize he has beaten the odds, done the impossible, risen above the fray of life and leads by example. I can easily see the fruit of his labor and the Jesus in him.

Mrs. Janice Ware

CHAPTER TWO

Good Leader, Poor Leader

GOOD LEADERS ARE not born, they are made. A good leader is God's manager. He is a faithful and blameless steward, conscious that he is managing God's resources and gifts and knowing he will have to give an account. Do you know what it takes to be a good leader? Let's take a quiz. Complete each sentence with the correct answer.

> 1. AS A LEADER, ONE OF THE FIRST THINGS YOU SHOULD DO IS:
>
>   A. Personally get to know each of your direct reports.
>
>   B. Learn to delegate.
>
>   C. Bring employees into your office for one-on-one meetings.

A typical person, a leader, that's starting a brand new job wants everybody to come in their office and talk to them. That is not the job of the leader. The answer is B: learn to delegate. You're there as a leader to get some work done. If you are blessed to have people work in that office and you are assigned a staff or what-have-you, your job is mainly to get things done through them. And so, learn to delegate is your answer.

Why would it be a bad idea to get to know them one-on-one? Number one: when you were hired by this company, they hire your gifts, your skills, your education, your academic success, and your experience to fulfill a mandate to meet product line goals and thereby profits. It's good to talk about your family, your marriage, your kids, "I'm sick," "going through," all of that, but that is not the job of the leader. You get sick days for that. When you're on your job and they say you're going to work forty hours, for those forty hours you need to be working. Also, the leader doesn't want to set a standard where people can just come in his office anytime they feel like they want to come in and talk. No. Go to your office. That's why we have the weekly meetings. If you have something that is pertinent, you go ahead and send an email of concern or you work with those particular leaders' secretaries to get on their schedule or agenda. And be specific about what you want. But the leader's job is to delegate work out, because he is responsible for absolutely everything. And if he doesn't delegate, and his boss—because everybody has a boss—or even the company owner wants to know, "Why we didn't make any money?" Delegation.

2. WHEN YOUR MINISTRY IS UNDER FIRE FROM UPPER MANAGEMENT:

   A. Act as a buffer.

   B. Find the problem and fix it.

   C. Stay cool.

The typical answer that most people would say would be B, to find the problem and fix the problem. The answer is really A. When you are under attack from upper management, and it is falling on you as a manager, and you have people working beneath you, act as a buffer. You have to absorb that issue; you've got to receive it because the bosses are right. You are responsible. So you can, in turn, stay cool and then try to go see the president to find out what is going on. You act as a buffer because many times upper management might not have a clear view or the picture perspective of what the workers are doing. And if they are working for you, and all you're doing is being a tyrant, when they (the bosses) come down on you, and you come down on them (workers), then the morale will not be there and they will lose some level of respect for you. So they have to have a balance. What you want to do is act as a buffer and being a buffer, you begin to allow the workers to continue to do what they are doing. The worst thing for a leader to do is to respond in kind, so as soon as he gets chewed out, to go down and chew out those who work for him. Jim Collins says, in his book, "Good to Great" that "the best leaders combine two oddly fitting characteristics—Humility and Tenacity, able to subordinate their egos to the need of the community. Their predominant driver is the mission not self."

> 3. LEADERS SHOULD RECOGNIZE THAT PEOPLE:
>   A. Thrive on praise and recognition.
>   B. Get bored if there is not enough work to do.
>   C. Will rise to the occasion if there is financial incentive.

Again, A is the answer. They thrive on praise and recognition. The majority of people I would say probably high, in the 80% range, are very conscientious of their work. They understand productivity is important and when they put their name on something, and they have an opportunity for the boss, the managers, and directors to say, "You know something? We appreciate you doing the work you're doing," that verbal praise, affirmation, appreciation goes a long way. It lets them know that their labor, their sacrifice, is truly not in vain. And everybody needs praise and recognition. I think that's an unalienable right of every human being that works for anybody.

What is the shortcoming of saying, they'll do it if you give them the money? Well, sometimes the money will not be there.

Sometimes the economic downturn come in and sometimes you have to tighten the belt financially to your office, to your department, and if you're only getting that motivation through financial rewards, you're just not there, well again, you're committing economic suicide.

> 4. AS A LEADER, IT IS NOT ACCEPTABLE TO:
>   A. Show empathy to the workers.
>   B. Lose your temper.
>   C. Write personal notes of appreciation.

It's B. As a leader you should never lose your temper. With leadership, you should be at the professional level in your ranks. There are a lot of things that's happening around you and around your employees. So when they look at a leader, the worst thing you can do is let something get so far under your skin that you lose it. Once you lose your temper then you are out of control, and that is not the ear mark of a leader and that's not in your job description to lose your temper. So definitely what is going to happen, upper management is going to call you to the office and that's not good. So you never want to lose your temper.

> 5. A LEADER'S PRIMARY RESPONSIBILITY IS TO:
>
>   A. Perform above expectations.
>
>   B. Set and meet yearly goals.
>
>   C. Accomplish tasks through other people.

It's C, accomplish tasks through other people because as a manager's director, you've already had your conversation with your director or your president and they have already told you what they want. And now your job is to go out and accomplish things through the gifts and skills of the people that are working with you and around you.

What is the benefit of looking at your task through other people? Well, it is important. The thing of it is, leadership comes in where you're pouring your gifts and skills through your directives, through your instructions, through the meetings that you have, and the ending product is going to be what you want it to be at the end of the day. And then you get some type of, not only recognition, but a sense that people are actually buying into your style of leadership, and they're listening to implement what you've given them to do. Typically, and I think it would be right that if I am a director over a department, the assumption is, I know your job as well as my job and I also know what the end product should look like. So if I give you instructions to do your job and I make sure I provide you the resources you need to get it done, well if you take the recipe and my instructions and you fulfill that, then joy will be in me and every time your name is mentioned, it will go down easy with me when it comes down to your evaluation, you're a team player. You follow orders. You can be trusted. I can give you a key to the restroom.

> 6. LEADERS SHOULD SPEND MOST OF THEIR TIME:
>   A. Checking on worker's performance.
>   B. Clarifying expectations from the pastoral staff.
>   C. Teaching.

If I have to run around checking on your work and performance and those kinds of things, then I don't need you working for me. I don't have time to do that. That would mean that I could do your job. The answer is C.

The main job of a leader, most of his time, is spent teaching, giving instructions. That goes without saying, because every opportunity is a teaching time. As a matter of fact, there's a story. It's a true story. You might have to look it up. It is about this individual that was working for a company in the sales department. And he was highly recommended. The bosses brought him in. He was a sharp guy. You know, they gave him his parameters and his budget. He ended up making a deal that cost the company a million dollars. He was shocked. Of course, the boss called him in and said, "Listen John, can you see me at 9:00 tomorrow morning in my office?" Well, this guy has already got his resume ready.

He's already got his resignation letter already intact. He's packed and telling his wife, "Listen, I lost my job."

He comes to the office for the 9:00 meeting. The owner is in there. He has got a couple of other people in there you know. When you got it like that, you say, "Oh, Jesus." Well, he comes in and they say, "Well, why don't you sit down?"

He says, "No, I know what this is. Here's my resignation."

And they say, "No, why don't you sit down."

The boss says, "You know what happened yesterday?"

"Yeah, I lost the company a million dollars."

"That's not the way I am looking at it. What happened yesterday, we spent a million dollars educating you."

That man went on in that company and eventually became the president of the company. Awesome story! Every time, everything is a teaching time, for a leader.

> 7. GOOD LEADERS:
>   A. Make decisions.
>   B. Spend social time with employees.
>   C. Argue their point of view.

The answer is A: Good leaders make decisions. And decisions are not based on popular opinion. Decisions are based on what is the right thing to do. Decisions are hard; they are cold; they are based on fact sometimes. And sometimes, many times, they are not really totally embraced automatically. But that's what leaders do. They make decisions. When there is something in the lower ranks that is going on and it comes to the leader, and they expect or look to the leader to make a decision. That's his job.

> 8. PEOPLE EASILY LOSE COMMITMENT WHEN LEADERS:
>   A. Change their moods.
>   B. Leave work early.
>   C. Keep their distance from the workers.

The answer is A. Mood swings are terrible and detrimental for a company, especially in the employee arena. If I have to say, "I don't know what kind of mood she is going to be in today," and that's the kind of atmosphere you have in the workplace, then you approach them quietly. It is not good because if you're nerved up, you've got butterflies, you're always on pins and needles, then you're not comfortable to do your work. The atmosphere that I like to be in is where people are laughing and having fun. They can settle in and get stuff done. And the pressure of it is self-imposed. I tell them to put pressure on themselves because that's what I do myself.

> 9. WHEN TEACHING SOMEONE A SKILL:
>
>   A. Accomplish the training off-site.
>
>   B. Reward his/her efforts.
>
>   C. Use a variety of teaching tools.

The answer is C: use a variety of teaching tools. Everybody learns a little different. Illustration is important. Teaching takes on many forms because teaching is actually 55% body language, 15% your communication, and the other small percentage is just the end result of them watching [you] from a distance. It's vitally important that you use every resource possible—from charts to graphs, PowerPoints, stories, illustrations—you know, just doing a variety of things. Also, what it does, it keeps your leadership fresh. And they will remember your unique gift of creativity, which I think leaders need to have.

> 10. AFTER IMPLEMENTING A MAJOR CHANGE, BE AWARE THAT:
>
>   A. 30 percent of your co-laborers will resist the change.
>
>   B. Your church may be taking unnecessary risk.
>
>   C. Most people will get onboard quickly.

Be advised that one-third of the people are going to say, "No, no, no," automatically. As a leader, if you ever think you're going to get 100% compliance across the board, with changes, you are sadly mistaken — no matter what field or industry you're in. The answer is A. Whether it's church, whether it's secular, people do not naturally embrace change. Change threatens levels of insecurity. The rumor of a merger... "Oh, Lord. I'm going to lose my job. I'm not for it."

In the Book of Titus, Paul left Titus in Crete to organize it and remedy the weaknesses there. There was definite opposition to his ministry, and there is a suggestion that he wanted to resign! As long as Christians are in the body of flesh, there will be problems in the churches. When these problems arise, the leader's job is not to hide them but face them honestly and prayerfully and settle them according to the word of God. The church is a body, and the pastor must occasionally be a spiritual physician and re-set some broken bones.

What can a leader do, going into a change, knowing that it's going to be resisted by a certain amount of people? What then is the recourse for the leader? I think the more you do on the front end regarding the potential change that is coming, the better. Because normally, leaders already have some insight that change is coming. And so typically, it's communicating that change with a level of compassion and reasoning that positions the intellect of those to understand truly why we're making this decision. That's a bigger piece of the total pie. Lack of communication causes the greatest amount of fear when change comes. Even if they don't embrace it, they can understand it. And eventually they'll be softened in trying to get in line with the direction in which we're going.

In learning to be a great leader, the first step is to be open to feedback about yourself as a leader and separate it from you the person. So are you a great leader? Or do you have the desire to become one? Remember, a great leader is someone who has a clear vision and can turn that vision into a vivid picture that others can see. When you speak about your vision, it should be with a passion you feel in your heart, a passion that creates so much enthusiasm that your team members will want to jump on board. When major decisions need to be made, you should encourage everyone to use the Q-CAT decision making system (as outlined by Executive Coach Patty Vogan, "Quick, Committed, Analytical, Thoughtful") and to be responsible for their actions. You should be continually assessing your own character and never stop growing, personally or professionally.

Good Leaders Needed

Whenever Christ sows the good seed (believers), Satan follows with counterfeit seed and with false teachers. In Crete, there were a group of people who contradicted the teachings of Paul. Paul even quoted a famous poet, Epimenides of Knossos, who described the Cretans as "liars, ferocious beasts, and idle gluttons." Instead, of using those names, the Jewish fables (legalism) and the commandments of men (traditionalism) are used today. We must constantly beware of false teachers.

In Matthew, when Jesus looked out on the crowds, he had compassion for them because they were "harassed and hopeless like sheep without a shepherd." Jesus said "the harvest is plentiful but the laborers are few. Pray to the Father and he will send out laborers (MATTHEW 9:36-38)." Good leaders are needed because most people find themselves wandering from one place to the next "like sheep without a shepherd," trying to find a good leader. Requisite virtues of good leaders include the ability to listen, cast vision, inspire, serve, sacrifice, connect, teach, confess, provide care and remain humble. These attributes do not come easily for sons of Adam and daughters of Eve. As Chuck Swindoll observes, "It is tough to find a person who holds a high position and yet is tender before God." Only through the power of the Holy Spirit and the Grace of God can we grow into mature leaders.

Poor Leaders in the Church

Let's travel again to the Book of Titus where Paul quotes a famous poet, Epimenides, who describes the Cretans as "liars, ferocious beasts, and idle gluttons. " How is Titus to treat these false leaders? Is he to unite with them and try to see their view point? Absolutely not! He must shut their mouths and rebuke them sharply (TITUS 1:13). Their motive was simply to get money and not to honor the Lord. False teachers profess one thing and practice another. They are denying Christ by their works, they are abominable and disobedient (TITUS 1:16).

We have false teachers attacking the church today. It is one thing for a person to hold to false doctrine because of ignorance, and quite another for him or her to hold on to it and teach it as God's truth. Ignorant people should be pitied and taught the truth. Deliberately false teachers should be rebuked and rejected.

Once the church compromises on the truth, the truth will be swallowed up in lies. False doctrines only lead to sickness in the Body of Christ.

What does the Bible say about poor leaders? Can they change?

I think about Saul versus David. Saul, in scripture, was a man of tall stature. The scriptures say he was a good looking man, and the Israelites chose Saul because they wanted a visible king. Samuel is the prophet communicating with God. God is speaking to Samuel to tell the people: Is God not enough? God is saying, "Am I not enough for you?" But, the Israelites are persistent, "Samuel, tell God we want a king. The Philistines have a king. We can see their king. We want a king." They chose Saul. What they did not know about Saul is that Saul was a coward when it came to Goliath. And so out of that [Israel's] poor leadership, the people called for Saul, so God gave them permission and it was so.

But God anointed David as King of Israel, as a little boy. And so, could Saul change? The possibilities, I do believe, are always there, but you've got to get to a point where you actually align your leadership with the Word of God. You have to be hearing from God. And you have to be sure enough to hear from God so that you can obey him, even against public opinion.

At the end of Saul's reign, David comes as a little boy, but a true king, and actually leads Saul. He was able to give Saul what Saul couldn't give to the Israelites: Goliath's head. And so from that situation, animosity built in, jealousy built in, rage built in to the point to where Saul wanted to kill David. Could he change? All things are possible with God. But if you are a poor leader, and you are unwilling to acknowledge your weaknesses and embrace another's strengths, you will always be a poor leader.

How do you overcome the influence of poor leaders?

Well, there are a couple of things — one or two things you have to remember. (1) You are not responsible for the results of another's leadership; (2) you are responsible for *the results of your* leadership. If there is something you can do to enhance that person do it. Sometimes when you have that natural *gift* of leadership, *very seldom* will you find yourself navigating behind a poor leader, because normally poor leaders and successful leaders very seldom do they intersect on the highway. Because poor leaders — there are a lot of them — they normally, typically hang with other leaders like themselves. Successful leaders, bona fide leaders, they normally hang with the crème of the crop.

I often ask individuals, "Are you an eagle, are you a chicken, or are you a pigeon?"

And everybody tells me, "I'm an eagle. My leadership is like an eagle."

But then, I go on and tell them, "Okay, let me give you a couple of things I want you to know…"

Let me tell you about the pigeon. The pigeon right here in Houston, Texas headlines over at Fiesta at West Belfort and Fondren. They are all in the parking lot they're flying, waiting on somebody to throw a piece of bread out so that they can grab it and eat and have some nourishment. And so, they walk right around you in the park, waiting for you to throw them some bread or something. That's the pigeons. The chickens headlines at several different places. You will see them when you get there. They are at Churchs Chicken, Chik-Fil-A, Popeye's, Timmy Chan's, and the Frenchy's in Third Ward, but they are going into the grease, so their life is limited. The *eagle,* unlike the pigeon or the chicken, does not eat on the ground. They don't even walk around on the ground. They are protected birds. As a matter of fact, they are an endangered species.

When I think about poor leadership, when people say they are eagles then I ask about the people you surround yourself with. Are they more of a chicken, pigeon, or mainly eagles? And if they hesitate for any amount of time, if they say, "You know something, I do have some pigeons and a couple of chickens around me." Then I say, "You know something, maybe you're not an eagle at all." Because eagles just don't hang with chickens and pigeons. When eagles come, they swoop in, they grab what they have to grab, and they go on up. Eagles are smart. They pair-off and mate for life. And they have enough sense to make their home on high.

Life Letter

Good leadership begins at the front door, with a warm smile to greet you as you enter the church. Your leadership style suggests that you are truly led by God and that your decisions will be God's way or no way. Having great ideas and bringing people together for a good cause is a great step toward being a successful leader.

There are individuals who consider themselves leaders and who have the ability to imagine great things and bring people together; but that's where their leadership ends. Pastor August has a servants' heart and works along-side us as he leads us. This is a rare quality that many never achieve. Honesty and integrity are also essential qualities of an effective leader. He also possesses the ability to delegate various tasks to others. This allows him to focus his attention on matters so that other areas of the ministry are not neglected. The time and energy that he devotes to ministry is seemingly inexhaustible. He has a sense of humor that turns things around at a moment's notice and just when it's most needed.

The demonstration of his faith propels us to do even greater works so that the lives of others will be impacted. His ability to inspire me and others is so amazing. I know only God equips him to do all that he does.

Poor leadership is contrary to the will of God. It destroys from the core and tears down what God desires to build. Over the course of my life I have experienced the effects of poor leadership and the devastation that it has on the entire church body. Leaders who are focused on self-gain and lack love for their congregation as well as "the least of these" will not accomplish anything eternal for the cause of Christ. The evidence will be apparent because there will be no growth in the people spiritually or the impact of their ministry in relation to their community.

Good leaders pull the future forward. Poor leaders are more concerned about survival than growth. Under poor leadership, the people have no vision.

ROBERT STANTON

CHAPTER THREE

Family Application

Fathers as Leaders

I REMEMBER WHEN I presided over the funeral of my step-father. He was really a dad to me, and this man did something so profound. He did something that I don't think many men would ever do. He married my mother who was already caring for eight children. This man was 26 years old when he took on a 33 year old woman with eight kids. That's a big thing to do at 26, 46, or any age. It's unheard of for men to do something like that. But that demonstrated level of love and sacrifice helped us, as children to see what was quality versus what we saw in quantity. We had what we needed.

We had models for learning how to fish, learning how to drive, work ethics—this man taught me all that. We were given the right substance as individuals versus having stuff that couldn't really help us build our character, build our integrity, and then fortify our relationship with God. And the blessing was, for his funeral, although he and my mom had been divorced for 20 years, all of my siblings showed up. It is a testament to what he did with us.

When we look at husbands and fathers, absenteeism leads to a lack of quality leadership. For single moms with children it's difficult, especially with boys. In every man, there is a dominant seed even as a little boy. This young man is not going to allow his mother to rule over him. And so the mother often caters to him as "her man," even in that young state. She dresses him up, fixes him up, and keeps him close, keeping him warm and groomed. The whole nine yards. Even while he is a grown man, she will still take care of him. But she will put a daughter out of the house the moment she starts mouthing off. But think of Samuel's mom, in the Bible, who prayed that God would bless her womb with a child. And the key of it is, when God blessed her and she got pregnant, she had said before, "If you bless me with a child, I will present him back to you." It is vitally important that single moms have this mind-frame. That was one of my mother's challenges. First of all, she had to get herself to Jesus by surrendering her life to Christ.

Being raised Catholic, her family went to mass, but having a real relationship with Christ just wasn't there. When she came into a real relationship with Jesus Christ and then she brought her kids into the presence of the Lord, that's where things began to change. First and foremost, the mother must get herself in Jesus, then align her kids in the face of Christ, and allow Christ to step in and become that father figure within that family. Then whatever is needed, God shall supply.

Sometimes in your single state, marriage might not happen while your kids are young. I mentioned how my step-father married my mother with eight kids. That's not going to happen anymore. That is a historical event. That is a miracle! That is like Jesus walking on the water. Right after he walked on water, my step-father married my mom.

So when you think about what you need to be doing, it's getting back to the principles and the base of God's Word. And if you do that, the Lord steps in and takes care of your children. We are all heavenly-made, and we have to know that. Mothers have to know that. Children have to know that. Fathers have to know that. You are heavenly-made because it's God who is the protector and the Creator of the womb. Read Psalms 139. You can bank on that.

Now, I don't want to take anything away from moms. Mothers, grandmothers, aunties, Big Momma, and them, they have all been great role-models over the years, doing all that they can. And here's the crazy thing, sometimes the least likely of persons can teach you leadership because of something that they're doing.

I think of the Underground Railroad with Harriet Tubman. This one woman was entrenched in slavery, poverty, and man's inhumanity to man. But she had the unction, after attaining her own freedom, to go back into the hell of slavery and take other people out of "hell" into the Promised Land. Then, on her journeys, she did not lose one person she rescued. We're not talking about traveling from Southwest Houston to downtown, which will take you five hours if you do some power-walking. We're talking about going through states, going through hostile territories, traveling at night, looking for safe houses with no maps and no navigation systems like what we have today. Nowadays, we have the key map and GPS. We can be anywhere we want to be just by having our iPad. Can you imagine going from place to place, traveling like Tubman and not losing one person? The qualities that Harriet Tubman showed and the dedication to what she was doing falls right in line with what needs to happen in the home with men. But fear plays a part in many failed role-models for the family, because to lead, it will cost you something. And many times, individuals are not willing to pay the price to be the leader.

I knew a guy once and he worked about 20 years for this one company. I asked him, "Why haven't you moved up?" And his answer to me kinda surprised me and startled me. He said, "I was offered some promotions, but I didn't take them. I don't want the extra work. I don't want the extra responsibility." The killing part to me is (and I'm embarrassed to say this but) he's a pastor! I don't understand that. God reveals these things, though, because sometimes we've been modeled under role-models that are broken—and no one told us. Leadership is something that you *do* verses just being a label. Leadership is earned and demonstrated where people can see it, without you saying that you are the leader.

Culturally, many of our young men and women are completely dismayed with our current crisis where leadership is lacking in the home. When Bethel's Family did a men's conference with about 30 men, we discovered that there's a lot of pain and hurt over the lack of leadership in the homes we grew up in (in my case, regarding the household, I was raised in without my biological father). A majority of these men grew up in situations similar to mine where they were without their fathers. We all grew up in different geographic areas, from Florida to California, coming from different walks of life. Even so, we were all experiencing some of the same stuff internally. We started talking about the death of our fathers, for those of us who could remember. Two young men shared stories where their fathers did not do anything in leadership, at all. And so, one man said, "At my father's funeral, nine people showed up." Nine. The other man said, "I can go one step further. There were six people at my daddy's funeral." How can you live in this land for sixty-plus years without impacting anybody's life in a positive way where they will miss you when you're gone? Failed leadership. It failed at home.

Leadership Starts at Home

Most people don't see themselves as leaders. Even as a parent, they don't recognize their leadership role. Truth is, you are a leader in more ways than one. Even if you're only overseeing your dog and cat, you are a leader in that home, because they are expecting you to show some diligence in how you treat them and how you run your home.

So, we begin to operate, bringing about what we call a masterpiece, with some of the pieces of the family puzzle on the table. However, the problem is, we have lost all of the pieces to the family blueprint. So now, people have a piecemeal they want to label as "good family practices" and "values." But when you look at culture, economics, social standing, and academia, you find a great gulf between leadership in the home and leadership on the street.

Take, for instance, the average drug dealer. He somehow takes care of everybody that works for him illegally on the street corner. They are accountable, even with their lives, when it comes to keeping the drug dealer in business. They have a silent code of ethics. If they do anything outside of that code, they could lose their lives—and many have lost their lives. Well, you take that leadership that's out in the street and you try to transfer that leadership into the home, and you get fathers and mothers in conflict.

The Word says, "Husbands, love your wives, just as Christ loved the church and gave himself up for her to make her holy, cleansing her by the washing with water through the word (EPHESIANS 5:25-28)." Many Christian husbands misunderstand their calling, seeing headship as making the decisions and controlling their wives. Many husbands abandon the call to cherish their own wives and to be the spiritual heads of the home. "Cherish," in the Greek, means to, literally, keep warm. But nowadays, there is an empty chair at the dinner table, an apathetic heart toward the things of God, and a cold unresponsiveness of men to the real needs of their wives and children. Husbands are called to cover their wives with protection and provision, as Christ does the church. But many husbands have covered their wives with violence, leaving them destitute. Ironically, these men still come to the altar with tearful pleas, expecting God to accept them and hear their prayers.

But Peter instructs husbands to "be considerate as you live with your wives, and treat them with respect as the weaker partner and as heirs with you of the gracious gift of life, so that nothing will hinder your prayers (1 PETER 3:7)." When I first read that, it scared me half to death. My wife would share with me, "Honey, you're not even considering me. You're my husband. You're my leader. And you don't even ask me what I'm thinking. You don't even include me." She was telling me that and I struggled with that. I'm smart; I've got some intellect. But imagine you're making a gumbo, and I feel like I can add something to this gumbo. I have all of the shrimp and sausage in this corner, and you have the other few ingredients. If you don't consult or consider me, I'm going to be less likely to hand over my shrimp and sausage. You can try to make do with what you have, but it would be a whole lot better if we add the ingredients that I bring to the table.

Called to Servant Leadership

Husbands are called to "servant leadership," which means that husbands are also called to be examples of Christ (EPHESIANS 5:1). When we think about husbands, we think about wives. Because the "husband" is a role that a man gets once he is joined to a woman in holy matrimony. It's a different role that the man needs to play. There are two forms of resemblance considering Christ to the Church and husband to wife:

1. A husband needs to love his wife, so much, just as he loves his own body.

    "In this same way, husbands ought to love their wives as their own bodies. He who loves his wife loves himself (EPH. 5:28)."

2. A husband needs to be willing to lay down his life so his wife can survive.

"Husbands, love your wives, just as Christ loved the church and gave himself up for her (Eph. 5:25)." Christ died for the church that the church might live.

We're living in a time where these pieces of the puzzle are fractured and now, it is the opposite situation. Now you have only women who are servant leaders to the men in their lives, and they're not getting anything in return. And that's where we have a disconnect. You have many unhappy wives and women who cannot find *suitable* men because they don't know how to correctly define a husband. Often, you get married and that's the end of the journey. You get the nice dress, the flowers, the cakes, the candy, and all the whistles and bells. You get married. Then on Monday, you go back to a normal state, and you're just living together. The only difference is, you have a piece of paper that says this past Saturday, you got married. That's not the original blueprint. Husbands and wives should be living in a state of servant leadership. As a servant leader with over 25 years of marriage, I'm finding myself serving my wife more than I've ever served her before.

Serving each other has nothing to do with "who is serving who." It's something you just do. It has to become a part of your DNA. Serving is what you *should* be doing—no strings attached.

Take Care of Home: Needs of Wives and Husbands

There are many books out there that talk about the differences between men and women, other than what's obvious. But there is a significant difference in the area of the basic needs of each gender in marriage:

1. The wife's basic need is for a godly spiritual leader. That's her number one basic need from her husband. On the other hand, a husband's first need is respect and affirmation, because men travel every day with our egos on our shoulders.

2. The wife's second need is affirmation and appreciation for even the little things she does. Nothing should compromise that. When you go back to the husband, his second need, after getting respect, is sex. If the wife can master those two needs of the husband (respect and sex), he will go ahead and give her the other four that she needs. But just for the record, respect is first. Sex is second.

3. Thirdly, the wife needs romance. Romance is not sexual, but it can lead there. Third for the husband is that he needs his wife to be attractive (fix her hair, diet, etc.).

4. Fourthly, the wife needs intimate conversation. She needs her husband to talk to her heart and listen to her heart. The

fourth thing a husband needs is home support. He can't work all day, come home, and have to struggle at home.

5. The fifth need of a wife is openness and honesty. Simple stuff. The woman is naturally built to handle the truth. It's the lies that mess her up. There's something about how God has designed women where they can handle the truth. We haven't learned to trust that yet. The truth might break her heart, but she will embrace that truth. And she will actually respect you because it is the truth. If you start lying, you will destroy her heart. She may stay with you for a long time, but she will never trust you. The last thing a husband needs is a life companion. Typically, the wife is going to out-live him. In other words, he's going to be in Depends diapers way before his wife. He's going to need someone to change him.

6. The sixth need of a wife is home support. She needs a husband who handles his business. She needs money coming in, available to her at all times. She needs the home to be stabilized, because she wants family to be first. She wants to put some biblical principles in the home and build traditions.

How sad it is that many husbands, who are not servant leaders, take care of everybody else's home except their own. Then his wife sees him walking around at church like he's "got it going on." You need to take care of home. And let me say this: sometimes as leaders, as husbands, our wives may have to go somewhere and leave the kids at home with us. One of the gravest mistakes we husbands make is in thinking, "I don't have time to babysit those kids." How can you say that? You don't babysit your own children. You *parent* your children. This misconception with fathers has been going on way too long. It should not be a chore. It ought to be a joy.

When you're called to leadership, it starts at home. And from home, it comes to the church. So, if you're not a leader at home, you shouldn't be a leader at church — especially if you are a man. It takes creative leadership and obedience to God's will to effectively manage and take care of your home.

Mankind's Moral Requirement

The presence in the garden of the tree of the knowledge of good and evil, in Genesis, chapter two, established a moral demand that rests upon humanity. God placed man in the garden and gave him the task of keeping it. If men will learn to trust the heart of God enough to go higher with him, they will find that He takes us higher in our marriage. A man cannot be spiritually in sync with his wife until he is in sync with God.

Just in general, every leader is called to be an example of Jesus Christ (Ephesians 5:2-2). When we talk about our example, our character, our behavior, who do we counsel with? Well, Christ already walked this earth for thirty-three and a half years. There are not any challenges that we're going to encounter that Christ has not already encountered and conquered. He's already paid the ultimate price that we might live. He's taught us how to love; how to forgive; how to be a good neighbor; how to be concerned about those who are the least, the lost, and the last.

Acknowledging his faithfulness to his Father and his consistency in dedicating himself to God's work and God's will, these are modeled examples of Christ. Paul says, live a life of love as Christ did (EPHESIANS 5:2), and we know there's no greater love than the love that Christ has given to us (JOHN 15:13). "But among you there must not be even a hint of sexual immorality, or of any kind of impurity, or greed, because these are improper for God's holy people (EPHESIANS 5:3)."

At the end of the day, when we look at ourselves in the mirror, we have to recognize that we can only be an instrument in the hands of the Lord. So, we should remove ourselves from the temptations of sexual immorality or anything that can put us in a distant relationship with God. As leaders, whenever we find ourselves going down that road and temptation besieges us, it's not because we were caught off-guard. No! According to James, when you are tempted, you cannot say God is tempting you because God tempts no man (1:13-15). "But each one is tempted by his own evil desire. And when his desire is conceived, it gives birth to sin. And when sin is full-grown, it gives birth to death." The reality is that there's temptation all around all the time. Simply, men, we must see little girls as our daughters. We must see young women as our sisters. We must see those in the middle-age and older as our elder sisters and mothers, and the other women either as our grandmothers or our great grandmothers. Too often, we are seeing girls and women in a light that only reminds us of our fleshly nature.

Paul says something else. In First Corinthians, he says, "I beat my body and bring it under subjection, so after I have taught other people, I myself will not be disqualified from the prize (1Cor. 9:27)." It's a constant battle each day. That's why, as leaders, we have to dedicate ourselves back to God every single day. Every single morning, when you look in the mirror, rededicate yourself to God's plan and God's will. Because when we sleep and slumber through the night, we find ourselves getting a little comatose. And sometimes, all of our marbles don't get off the pillow.

I'll give you the example of King David. David should have been on the battlefield with Uriah, instead of sleeping with Uriah's wife, Bathsheba. He missed out on opportunities, and because of that, he found himself going through some challenges and turmoil. And his children suffered because of his decision to sleep with Bathsheba. He found himself being divorced from the power, the presence, and the peace of a good God. All of Psalm 51 is David's song of repenting, his pleading for God to take him back, and his cry that God would restore him. And God did do that, but God shared with him, because you have shed blood and sinned this way, I cannot use you to build my temple. However, God gave him the privilege of gathering the materials. Then, God used Solomon, David's son with Bathsheba, to build His temple.

We All Make Mistakes

The truth is, all fathers make mistakes. We just have to trust God and learn from our failings. Once you leave home, then you're in a different lifestyle, economically. Your rent is three times higher than your mother's mortgage. You've got a car note, so you need money to live. But the frightening part for me was that when you grow up with meager beginnings, you never want to go back. I always said, whether I fail or succeed, I would never fail in the presence of my mother because I never wanted to break her heart." So, working was how I made money. The more work I can put on my plate, the more money I can make. That's how I thought in that process. As a matter of fact, when Sister August met me, I had three jobs. I was working at the bank 40 hours, plus I did overtime. I worked at that bank for nine and a half years without missing one day of work. I had my own landscaping company with a buddy of mine, and we did that on weekends. And I, also, answered after-hour ATM alarm calls. Why? I wanted to make sure I was never laid off without a job. That's why. But it put some hardship on family, on marriage, on kids because I was always ripping and running. That's the downside.

Fathers Making the Right Choices: The Story of Noah

I've noticed that people will break the bank for Mother's Day, but they get fickle on Father's Day. It's good to celebrate fathers in a land where we find so many reasons *not* to honor the father. I don't know the community or neighborhood or the place where you work, but I got to tell you something, when you open up your eyes and look around it seems as though we don't have enough men making the right decisions in difficult times. Believe it or not, the man, the husband, the father is the one that needs to have the model leadership for the whole family. We have too many fathers who are not anointed and appointed to stand. For whatever reason they find themselves unable to be the fathers that God called them to be. Regardless of the situation, if that's you, stand and be a father. There are no excuses for a man with a child. You must be a father to that child.

However, when we talk about fathers making the right choices, I think of Noah, a father who lived in difficult times. Noah learned to make the difficult choices in times of crisis. Noah was dealing with some of the same problems that we're dealing with today. And in the Book of Genesis you see that man has always had a desire and a nature to do what he wants to do. In Noah's days there were no men really seeking God. There were no men conducting Bible studies in their home. There were no men praying before a meal. They all had a desire to do what they wanted to do and they said, "This is my life."

With the story of Noah, many of you know about the ark and the animals and all that, but let's look at the man, Noah, and his circumstances. Noah had a wife and three sons. Genesis 6: 9 -12 says, *"Now the earth was corrupt in God's sight and full of violence. God saw how corrupt the earth had become, for all the people on earth had corrupted their ways."* And when you look at our culture in Houston doesn't it seem as though we're dealing with the same picture that God saw in Genesis, chapter six? Noah was living in the same times, same pressure. Men were doing what they wanted to do, living the way they wanted to live. They were not concerned about following the pecking order of God. Men were able in their own spirit to try and justify their own lives. But *"Noah was a righteous man, blameless among the people of his time, and he walked with God."*

Today, we look at fathers as men of strength, men of purpose, men of destiny. When a woman takes a man's name she is symbolically saying, "lead me." She's saying, "I want you to have purpose and vision. I want you to have a plan for the family. I'm going to place my life under your authority, so make sure I'm safe. Make sure you build a house where I can rest, where I have peace, and where you can have food, so when you're hungry I can go to the cupboard and refrigerator. And I can put it together the things you bought and make you happy. If you do all that and keep the bills paid; keep me riding good and looking good and smelling good, later, at night, you'll be rewarded." That's what she's saying.

So, Noah had the responsibility of maintaining his family in a world when people would rather walk a dog than walk their child. I see so many men walking pitbulls and rottweilers and while their children are languishing with no food and no shoes. What's wrong with that picture? They take their rottweilers to the hospital and stay up all night long while the pitbull has puppies. Something is wrong with that picture.

So when God looked upon the earth God saw the corruptness of mans' heart. He saw the wickedness that lay in mans' life. He saw the violence that's been around for a long time. But God hated it then, and he hates it now. There are crimes against humanity; men against men, mothers against fathers and daughters and so on. God doesn't like that. Domestic abuse is at an all-time high. Men don't know that their hands, their fists, are not made to go upon a woman's head or body or mouth. Your hands were made to work hard. And when you are out of control, this world wants to put you in bondage. So all of this calamity and corruption is the reason why we have to build more and more prisons. But Noah decided to be different.

Decide to be Different

Noah was a righteous man, blameless amongst the people of his time. And I want you to know, brothers, that there comes a time when you have to be different. Noah had some choices to make. He could have decided to look like the rest of the brothers. He could have decided to neglect his family. He could have decided against achieving the thing that God instructed him to do. He could have said, "That's just the way it is." But no; he had to be different.

Even though there was corruption in the land, God had a plan. Noah, as a father, receives God's instructions to *"make yourself an ark of cypress wood; make rooms in it and coat it with pitch inside and out. This is how you are to build it: The ark is to be 450 feet long, 75 feet wide and 45 feet high."* God designed the ark. And 450 feet is about a football field and a half. God knew what he was doing. At those measurements, the ark would not flip over. A mighty flood was coming. The event changed history forever, because everybody perished who was not on the ark.

Well, we are living in the land where people are perishing. And they're perishing in droves. We are dying because of the lack of education. We're dying because we're not seeking the kind of employment to build prosperity in our own family heritage. We're lacking in economic power because we haven't learned to work together. We're majoring in incarceration. AIDS, HIV, and all kinds of health issues are plaguing our community. We're not owning anything; we're leasing stuff. And, we are lacking in parenting skills. The same parenting system that our mothers and grandmothers used, we have put that on the shelf because now we have a new order.

We're losing people to the streets. Negative media and gangs are busy. Drugs are everywhere. The "absent father syndrome" can spread its seeds all over the community: crime, violence, and death. There's something God wants to show us here. If we don't make the right decisions in difficult times, don't you know, whatever we do not complete it'll fall upon our children and grandchildren? And it's going to be much harder for them. So in a corrupt situation, Noah decided to be righteous.

Receive God's Instruction

The second thing: Noah received God's instructions. And when you look at him receiving God's instructions he did exactly what God said to do. This ark was made by God, designed by God, and he built it by God's specifications, and God only put one door in it. God said, "You just go ahead and follow my instructions. You get two of every kind of species in it, and then you get your family in it. Once I get ready, I'll let the rain come, but I will close the ark door." I thought about that. Why wouldn't God give Noah the authority to close the door? And it came to me while I was sleeping.

I woke up in a cold sweat. God didn't give Noah the power to close the ark door, because he knew the floods would come and there would be folks from South Park saying, "hey, let me in Noah!" And Noah would have opened the door. God said, no. It took Noah 120 years to build the ark, and God was giving the people time to get their lives right. I do believe, right now, God is giving us time to get right. Somebody ought to say, "Amen." The reason why he hasn't annihilated what you've got going on is because He's giving you time to get right. The time is at hand.

Noah understood that his blessings are in following the instructions that the Lord was putting in his life. Some of us, when we get the instructions from God, we want to gather with folks and say, "what do you think about this?" But Noah did not have a town hall meeting. He did not call the community together. Noah heard from God, received instructions from God, and he had faith in what God told him to do.

Do you remember Hurricane Katrina? Remember looking at the pictures of this mighty hurricane and the devastation it caused to a lot of our family and friends and others in the Gulf Coast region. You were watching the television and you saw a storm, but imagine 40 days and 40 nights of torrential rain. If it just rained for 24 hours straight, in Houston, half of the city would be flooded. Think about 40 days and 40 nights. God said, "I'm going to destroy every living thing that's not in the ark." And it doesn't matter what you're doing. It doesn't matter where you are. It doesn't matter what you have. It's going to be so terrible that even the very little boat that you have won't make it.

Learn to Obey

One of the things I share with fathers: learn to obey God. I got an email one night and I have to paraphrase it because I can't remember it verbatim. It came from a woman. The woman said, "Pastor August, I was at Bible study on Wednesday night when we ran the bases and talked about being in position. We do want to follow the men, but, pastor, they've got to be leading us. They've got to have a purpose and a destination. They've got to have a plan, pastor. We can't just get behind anybody." My heart's sentiments went with her and what she said was already validated earlier that day. I had my three sons and we went to a men's conference. At the men's conference of course we learned a lot of things about the order of God and most men struggle with obeying God. They just struggle with God's word, and they end up living painful lives; unnecessarily living painfully with their children. We've got to learn to follow God's instructions because it's not good to have people view us in a negative context even though we have money in our pockets and we're all right. That's why I want to give you some new orders.

Order #1: Value Knowledge and Spiritual Stability

Number one, brothers: embrace reading. While you're waiting on something else, read. Thirst after knowledge. You've got to read more than the sports section. Ebony and Jet are good, but diversify your reading material so that no matter what room you step into, you belong in that room because you know what you know. Once you know what you know, nobody can put you out. But if you don't know anything then you're already out. Teach all men to become positive role models to every other man.

Teach all men to have a firm spiritual foundation to create a stable home environment. Home is a place of peace and refuge. The temperature in your household should be your temperature. There ought to be joy in the home because you're there. With a firm spiritual foundation, when you thirst for knowledge, don't let the word of God leave you. If somewhere along the line you've given your authority over to your wife or to a child or somebody, you can reclaim it by standing back on the word of God. When you stand back on the word of God, the woman will be more than happy to relinquish leadership to you, but she's not going to give it back to you when you're inconsistent with your walk with God. So, walk with God. It's never too late to regain your leadership position.

Order #2: Dress Yourself

Teach men how to dress. A lot of you are professionals. Don't lower the standard because Snoop says you have to walk around holding your pants. We have to dress the way mom and dad taught us how to dress. We have to put on our clothes so we don't become a spectacle. When people look at us, they get nervous. It's not that the person, the boy or girl, is bad because they wear their pants like that, but that's the signal that it gives. It's negative.

Now if you're cutting the grass, brothers and you're running around the house doing errands that's fine. But when you step out of the house, get you a white suit and some red and white shoes and you go to the Post Office and mail your letter. Let them know you're coming out. As a matter of fact, when you dress well you get treated better. So wear your best stuff when you step out — men and women.

At the same time, we have to teach all men to control what the modern media does to a person's life. I don't dress based on what they wearing in Hollywood. I don't look at television and see a

Snoop, Fifty Cent, or any of the other fools. I don't even watch how other preachers dress. I'm a very conservative guy. I don't want to be a spectacle. I don't want to stand out. I just want to be a normal guy. When I've done what God says to do, I'm going to sit down and I'll blend right back into the crowd. If Satan comes in here he might grab a well-dressed brother, and think he's the preacher. But I'm in the crowd.

Order #3: Give Respect

Teach all men to respect every female; the young and the mature. Encourage every young woman, every young girl, respect her. Respect the sisters. When we start giving our sisters their respect and their due, the respect from them will return. Don't curse what you love. Don't beat what you say you're committed to. You can't force her to do anything just like God won't force you to do anything. Lead by influence and be an example. Also, don't let any other brother disrespect a woman. Teach him that it's not positive and that he curses his own life when he put down a woman because the woman carries the seed of the next generation. So family, be mindful.

Earn Your Reward

The final thing I want you to see about Noah is that he is rewarded. When you obey you're going to get rewarded. Look here in Genesis:

> "Then God blessed Noah and his sons, saying to them, 'Be fruitful and increase in number and fill the earth.

> The fear and dread of you will fall upon all the beasts of the earth and all the birds of the air, upon every creature that moves along the ground, and upon all the fish of the sea; they are given into your hands. Everything that lives and moves will be food for you. Just as I gave you the green plants, I now give you everything (9:1-3)."

Fathers and brothers, making the right choices in difficult times is a part of receiving the blessings which you're due. Noah, the story about Noah is because he obeyed God. He lived. His wife, whom he loved, lived. His three sons lived. His three daughter-in-laws lived. God used them to replenish the earth. You see, your obedience will bless not only you, your immediate family, but it will bless generations to come, when you obey.

Fathers Reconnect

Father's Day is a special day; a challenging day to begin to look at who you are, because you are not what you say, but you *are* what you do. When anybody grades you or gives you a report card it's not about what you said you were going to do. Your report card is the accumulation of what you have done; the active work that you've done and turned in. That becomes your final grade. But my brothers I need you to look and really see deep down on the inside if you've been disconnected from your children for whatever reason. If so, reconnect.

Do not complain about child support. Don't complain; give it. As a matter of fact, give a little bit more than what they're asking for. Let them know that you're not going to let any money separate you from your children. Hear what I'm saying because if you just obey God you won't even have to work a second job. When you take care of yours, God will definitely take care of His. God has promised to take care of His own, and you belong to Him. Don't worry about what the woman does. Your rewards are based on *your* obedience to the father. Get reconnected to your children, It doesn't matter their age. If you need to go and apologize to your grown children, do it so it can heal their heart, so they can be able to bring you the grandchildren you need to see. Before too long they'll say, "I've mended my relationship with my dad," and they're not going to hold you responsible for what was out of your control. They're going to be able to say, "Dad I forgive you."

Now, like me, your father may never do that for you, but don't allow it. Let the change start with you. Your dad could have never told you he loved you. He could have walked out on your mother even before you were born. Don't let that become your blockage.

Say, "My dad will account for his situation with God himself, but *my* children are going to get to know who I am. I know their mother and I have a strained relationship, but I'm going to let her know that I love my children and I want to be a part of their lives. I don't want to be somebody they don't know. I want to be an active part of their lives because I'm a real father and I'm going to trust God.

"I know he's going to provide what I don't have because when I start obeying God's word God will not only give me the desires of my heart, but he will also bless my children. Amen." Dads, reconnect.

Moms, if I can give you any message of warning, please do not poison the children's heart against their fathers. Don't do that. Allow that child to get to know his or her dad personally. If you're mad and angry because you didn't stay together and he did you wrong, take that up with God. Decide not to put that on your children. That way, they don't treat their fathers in a negative way when the problem is not their father.

Brothers, I'm calling you to come together. I'm calling for a gathering of the men to come together so we can begin to pray and cry out to the Lord and ask the Lord to heal our broken hearts, to ask the Lord to replace love and patience and kindness and forgiveness and grace and leadership back into our spirits. Ask God to unify the men in the body so that when God disperses us back out to our communities, we can be blessed men in our homes. Our wives will look up and say, "Here comes the man of the house, children. Let's all stand up." When the man walks in the house, they'll say, "Dad's here. Amen. Amen." Order comes to the home. So brothers when you hear pastor give a call, let's come and let God work on us. Amen.

Life Letters

God led many families to a small church off of Fondren Road on the southwest side of Houston, Texas, to The Church at Bethel's Family and Walter August, Senior Pastor. I thought to myself, "Wow, the church name has the word *FAMILY* in it, so this has to be the place God wants my family." I knew this was where God wanted my family to work and worship.

Pastor August spoke often of "family" in his sermons, but his passion for children is what drew me initially. When my family first moved our membership, there were struggles in my marriage. The messages of love, forgiveness, and the importance of family was strength to me. At times it seemed as if God was speaking directly to me through Pastor August.

Donna Beck

Pastor August ministers to all of God's children from every walk of life and in every available moment. Under the pastorate of Walter August Jr., my family knows to put God first in our lives. Pastor August often illustrates how God moves. I can truly testify to this fact. My family has grown spiritually and continues to grow under the leadership of Pastor August. I thank God for this blessing. I thank my pastor for the support and caring he has provided to my family and me over the years. I thank God for providing us with an example of a "good shepherd." At the Church of Bethel's Family, we know this "good shepherd" as Pastor Walter August, a man of God.

Sandra Sherrod

Pastor August taught me to establish my own relationship with my Father God. Then I'm able to conduct a relationship with my spouse, and I can work on a healthy and happy family! These are good steps for families to follow. I watch how Pastor addresses and speaks of his wife, his kids, his grandkids. I hear how he consistently works with the men in our church to be stronger men and how men should address women. Pastor says that a man should be the head of his house. That man should cover their wives and that a man is the prince and the priest of his home. He's teaching men how to keep and regain their families!

I thank God for providing a pastor that teaches! Pastor would say, "Just make it plain. Don't take me around the barn!" Yes, it took me a long time to receive understanding. I'm thankful, and I'll continue to strive with the help of the Lord to get my family right, amen!

GAYLE THOMAS

CHAPTER FOUR

Having the Right Priorities

AS WE BEGIN to look around, there is serious issue with all of us: we have to guard ourselves against having a greedy spirit. In this land, a lot of the confusion and conflict is because the "haves" don't want to share with the "have-nots." Even in our nation's capital this is a problem. But in the 12th chapter of Luke, Jesus and a man are in the crowd. They don't give the man's name, but he yells out to Jesus, saying, "Tell my brother to share the inheritance with me."

Jesus replied, "Man, who made me a judge or an arbiter between you two?"

He says here, very candidly, you have to watch out and be on guard for all kinds of greed. He was sharing with them that a man's life does not consist of his possessions. It is so very important to understand this because a lot of people lose their joy, love, and relationships. They lose sleep, all because they're wrapped up in the things of this world. But this world cannot give you the peace, the love, the joy that only can come from having the right relationship and the right priorities with the Lord. When you understand the story, if somebody gives you an inheritance that means that that person either worked and labored and was blessed, or they also received an inheritance and they're passing it down. It ought to tell you something. The thing that they had accumulated, they thought it was theirs too. So you must understand, you'll only become a co-manager of whatever the Lord provides. Jesus wanted to help the man understand what he was talking about, so he told this parable:

> The ground of a rich man produced a good crop. He thought to himself, What shall I do? I have no place to store my crops. Then he said, this is what I will do. I will tear down my barns and build bigger ones, and there I will store all my grain and goods. And I'll say to myself, You have plenty of good things laid up for many years. Take life easy; eat, drink and be merry (LUKE 12:16-21).

Now this man already had barns of vats that were completely filled. He has another harvest in the field that is in abundance, an overflow of what he already had. Instead of him looking around to see who else, maybe a neighbor, maybe somebody in the family that has a need...no. He didn't think about those that were suffering. He didn't think about those with no shoes on their feet. He was all about himself. Don't you know some folks like that? If it's not about them they're not getting involved and they have an abundance of stuff.

There was a real estate mogul, previously listed in Forbes wealthiest people, worth one billion dollars, but now he's in jail for fraud. How many millions do you need until you're satisfied, when you have people that are sleeping in the streets, people with nothing, people that need money for kids to go to college, elderly who need medication? But, the spirit of greed gets in and then you want more. How much more do you need when there are needy folks all around you? The spirit of "me, myself, and I" is killing families. It doesn't matter how much you have. You can have only ten dollars and still be greedy.

I remember, there was a time one of my sisters, and her family, was struggling. They did not have a vehicle, so they would ride the church bus to church. Before they left for church, my sister had gotten up that morning and all she had left was four chicken wings, some sweet peas, and a little rice. She cooked that little bit of food, so that when they got back from church, her husband, her daughter, and herself could sit down to eat. She'd give him two wings, give herself a wing, give my niece a wing, eat a little sweet peas, a little rice, and say thank you, Jesus. But that brother, her husband, instead of waiting on the church bus to go home, he caught a ride. Got to the house, ate the four wings and ate most of the rice and the sweet peas too.

When my sister and my niece got off the bus and came in the house, that brother was already in bed, and that broke my sister's heart. He didn't even think about his child. He knew that was all they had. He was thinking about himself. She eventually divorced him. But the reality of this story is, he did not even consider his child or his wife; it was all about him.

But God says to the greedy man in Luke 12, verse 20: *"You fool! This very night your life will be demanded from you. Then who will get what you have prepared for yourself?" This is how it will be with anyone who stores up things for himself but is not rich toward God."* God called this man a fool.

Who Controls the Future?

My mother was talking to a neighbor outside, cause back in South Louisiana they did not have fences like we have here. You could walk in the backyard to everybody's house, and so my mother would be out there hanging her clothes with the clothespin and the neighbors would be out there talking. As they end the conversation they would say, "Baby, I'll see you tomorrow, if the Lord say the same." They had enough sense to realize that they could not bring in another day unless God wills it. Even if you talk to her today she'll say, "Baby I'll talk to later if the Lord says the same." But this man in the story (LUKE 12:20) did not have enough sense to realize that he did not control the future and that's why God said, "you fool."

You've got all these plans about what you're going to do for yourself and this very night you could be getting ready to die. Who would get what you have? The point is, you've got to keep everything in its proper perspective. Life is fickle. Life is fast. It's very important to understand that God watches everything and everybody. And if God blesses you many times he's blessing you not just for yourself, but that you might be a bigger blessing in somebody else's life. If the truth was told, you didn't make it by yourself. Somebody else paid a price so you could have what you have right now. You've got to guard against this world and this gravity that pulls you into the spirit of being greedy. You've got to be careful because this greedy spirit can destroy your spirit.

Putting God first

Further in the same 12th chapter of Luke, in verse 31, Jesus says, *"But seek his kingdom, and these things will be given to you as well."* He says, *"Do not be afraid, little flock, for your Father has been pleased to give you the kingdom."* Jesus is saying, "I already know what you need before you even ask, and all I'm asking you to do is to keep me first."

Let me help you here. At a marriage conference, I was speaking to about eight couples and I said, "Listen, the most important thing in my life is God. The number one thing in my life that I don't play with—I don't move it around—is God." He wakes me up every morning. He starts me on my way. He gave me eyes to see, ears to hear, a mouth to talk, legs to walk, hands to clap. God is number one. He's keeping the blood running through my veins right now. He let me wake up this morning. God is number one. When I get sick he's the healer. He'll touch my body and get me off of the hospital gurney. When my money runs low, it's God who supplies a roof over my head, clothing on my back. It's God. So God is number one.

Second is my wife; Sister August is number two. My children are number three. I'm number four. You've got to make sure you have the right priorities because many times many of you are not experiencing the overflow of God because your priorities are all out of whack.

Years ago when we used to watch Soul Train they would have this little scrambling board. You remember that scrambling board where you have to figure out who the artist was or who the group was? One day I was watching that and they had this fellow on there and I could tell he was older than all the rest of the other dancers. He shouldn't have been on there. I don't know who he was or how he got on there, but that brother was old and he was at the scrambling board. And it should have been an easy, easy, easy, easy, easy group to guess. And then the song came on. It was called, "Float On," by The Floaters. Do you remember that song? That was their only hit. How can you miss that one? This brother was out there trying to figure it out and everybody was saying, "Floaters, Floaters!" And he was looking at it, moving letters around. That's how many of you are about your priorities.

People are trying to tell you to get it right. "God, God, God! Get it right!" It's not your work. It's not your job. It's not your boss. It's not your neighbor. It's not your co-workers. It's God. And when you've put anything in God's chair you need to be nervous because we serve a jealous God. Amen. He doesn't like to be played with. You're either going to love him and put him first in everything or not. First in your living. First in your giving. First in your work. First in everything. So when you go to your job tomorrow morning you are a Christian going to your job. You're putting God first, because if you are there, God is there. If he's first in your life, you're going to talk a little different; you're going to walk a little different; you're going to love a little different, when he's first in your life. There are some things you're not going to do when he's first in your life. Then he says, in Luke, "I'll give you these things" because that's his heart to bless you and give to you, but it's based on the alignment of keeping your priorities in check. Putting Him first.

Now here's a thing that makes a sad man go home and cry. *"Sell your possessions and give to the poor* (Luke 12:33)." See, that's the struggle we having right now in our nation, in our industry, in healthcare reform. The *have's* don't want to share with the *have-not's*. "I don't want to be pulling from what I have to give you some medicine to make you feel better. No, no, no, this medicine is for me and my family. I don't care if you don't have enough money. That's your problem."

Marvin Zinler used to say, "it's rough to be poor." He used to say it every time he would come off his newscast. And so we have this division.

But Jesus tells this man to go and sell your possessions and give it to the poor. "Lord, Lord, Lord. Jesus, listen, I'll follow you. I'll pray. I'll even sing in the choir. I'll usher. I'll preach your gospel. I'll do the parking lot ministry. I'll even join the greeters too. I'll work with the youth. You know, I'll do whatever you want me to do, but don't make me, don't even ask me, to sell what I have and give it to the poor." That's a hard lesson, but look what he says, *"Provide purses for yourselves that will not wear out, a treasure in heaven that will not be exhausted, where no thief comes near and no moth destroys. For where your treasure is, there your heart will also be* (Luke 12:33b-34)." Jesus understands; "I know exactly where you are." This is where you have to really understand. You've got to begin to call those things that are false god, false gods. If you have anything that you love more than you love God it's an idol and it's a false god and it's been placed there not by God, but by Satan.

And family believe it or not, when you think about this hard task, selling what you have to give to somebody else who has a need, I want you to know the blessing about having the right priorities, God first. Jesus says the poor will always be with you. There will always be people who are poor here. One of the things they used to do when we were back at home, especially those who were raised on the farm, all the greens and whatever vegetables in the neighborhood, if somebody needed something, they came and picked greens. They came and got fresh tomatoes. On those cold mornings when they killed that 800 pound hog that's been in the pen for two or three weeks being cleaned out, the men came from the community and they helped take him down and clean him up. Everybody left with some meat. Everybody left with some cracklings. They didn't have to pay anything. They shared with one another based on if they had need. If somebody's house burnt down everybody would come and pitch in to help to rebuild. Whatever was needed to help that family. They had a sharing spirit.

We have to get back to realizing there are some truths about what you have, you're only a breath away from, not having. Even with the abundance it still doesn't belong to you. I'm reminded of that. The other thing is that you don't ever have to be jealous of anybody else. God is an equal blessing God. Don't allow yourself to get caught up in the things in this world because all those things will rust and be destroyed, but the things eternal are the things that matter most. How you give your heart away, how you serve and how you make yourself a blessing to individuals, these are the things that matter most to God. All the rest of the stuff, he'll just throw it around to you and let you enjoy it for a little while. That's all it is. Never own anything. Enjoy it while you have it. Be a blessing while you have it because one of the things I've learned is, if God be for you, it's more than the world against you.

David said it like this, "I've been young, but now I'm old and I've never seen the righteous forsaken or their seed begging bread (PSALM 37:25)." You don't have to worry about your kids going hungry or your kids being homeless. No. What you *do* makes the difference for generations to come. Your faithfulness, your stewardship, your commitment to God makes all the difference cause many of us are here based on the faithful service of others in our family before us. Many of us are here on pure grace and mercy. Amen.

Always be mindful to get your priorities in order. Keep them straight. Guard yourself from having a greedy spirit. Be extra careful when you have it all. Keep the proper perspective in place. Seeking God's kingdom is number one. When you concentrate and you focus, focus on the things that have an eternal mandate. That lasts forever. The thing that lasts forever is our God, our Jesus, our Holy Spirit, the Eternal One, the heavens and the glory. And so when I invest, when I sow, I sow into eternity where the blessings continue to flow.

One of the things I also know, the God that I serve He did not change for my mother. The God that I serve did not change for my grandmother. He did not change for my great-grandmother, and He did not change from the generation previous to her. And I got the same news; He's not going to change for me, He's not going to change for my sons. He's not going to change for my grandchildren because He will be the same. He's the same God. What I'm sharing with you is this: the same message that was taught over 2000 years ago is still valid today. If you get your heart caught up into trying to gain this whole world and you forfeit your very own soul, your life has been all for naught. Don't get it twisted. Enjoy it, celebrate it, and share it. Enjoy it, celebrate it, and share it. You got a new house? Enjoy it. Celebrate it. Share it. Got a new car? Enjoy it, celebrate it, and share it. Got some fine china? We're holding onto stuff. We don't use that until special company comes. Jesus is not going to come back to eat with you. You'd better break out that fine china. Put some red beans and rice and greens and cornbread on that china. Everything in your house ought to be used. Think about it. All that fine china sitting up there.

Have the Courage To Say NO, When Everyone Else Is Saying YES

Joseph was a man who faced great temptations when he was put in charge of an official's house in Egypt, where the official's wife tempted him with sexually immoral behavior. But he refused. "With me in charge, " he told her, "my master does not concern himself with anything in the house; everything he owns he has entrusted to my care. No one is greater in this house that I am.

My master has withheld nothing from me except you, because you are his wife. How then could I do such a wicked thing and sin against God?" (Genesis 39:8-9).

Joseph fled the house after courageously saying, "no." People, just say NO! Family, may God help young people and their parents to be remembered for standing out and standing firm in the day of pressure to conform.

There was a terrible accident in the south several years ago, when a church bus returning from an outing was run into head-on by a drunk driver. Twenty-seven people died, including three adults. The driver of the other vehicle said he had been to a party and was pressured to drink and could not stop once he started. That decision cost the lives of 27 people.

I don't care how strong a Christian you are; peer pressure today is so intense that you cannot cope with it apart from the Lord. Shadrach, Meshach, and Abenego are models for depending upon God when the heat is on. When everybody in Babylon was bowing down to the king's idols, these three refused (Daniel 3:16-18). Their dependence was on God alone, and He delivered them. Every time you decide for God and for good, you build something in your inward character that will strengthen you to be who you ought to be before God. And the reverse is also true.

Don't Underestimate the importance of Your Choices

We know that every choice, good or bad, will have consequences. We have to spend a lot of time in prayer as we make choices because there will be some level of fall out. You're never going to have 100% of people to agree with you on every choice you make. If that happens, then the people who are making these choices can't value too much about what they're doing. Sometimes as leaders, we don't think things all the way through. And God knows, I've been guilty of this. That's why I know the importance of my choices. Sometimes we think, "Well it doesn't make any difference. It is just one person's decision. "

I think about Caleb. Take a moment and imagine every enemy of God occupying the land that God said he will give to you. You have a limited amount of people and resources. And you go to a place, and see your enemies there. I think about that episode in Numbers 13, when the spies were sent out to go ahead and survey the land. And many were sent out along with Caleb and Joshua to go ahead and scout out the promise land. Well, in the promised land, Canaan, the enemies of God lived in large numbers. When they came back to Moses, out of the eleven that went, only Caleb and Joshua felt in their heart that they could claim the land and have victory (NUMBERS 13:30-31). Here is a message for young people: the majority is wrong just as often as the majority is right. And especially during the teen years, the majority often makes very bad decisions. The other spies came back and said "Listen there's too many of them. They're going to squash us. They're going to kill us. We're going to be destroyed." And so, one wrong decision ruined a whole generation. Because of Israel's choice to listen to the majority of the spies, an entire generation of Israelites wandered in the wilderness for forty years.

We read that Caleb and Joshua said, "We can do this!" They had a spirit of optimism—a belief that 'God is with us'. Moses saw something in them that the other ones couldn't see in themselves. Caleb and Joshua realized, "if God has led us this far, he's not going to leave us right now."

Many times as leaders, we get amnesia quickly. God travels with us. God blesses us. God opens up doors for us. God opened the Red Sea up. God smote your former enemies. You saw them destroyed in the Red Sea. You get to the promised land, and then you forget that you're serving an Almighty God. Caleb and Joshua did not forget. So much so, that because they remembered, God eventually gave them victory. Now look at what happened: out of all the people that were with Moses, other than Joshua and Caleb, their generation and older all died off. They died because of their unbelief; because they couldn't see it; because of their own fear and inabilities to dream and believe that God could give them what his word says. He had already promised the land to them. But they ended up forfeiting an opportunity to go into the promised land because they didn't believe. Only Caleb and Joshua believed.

When Moses was laid to rest God took that same Joshua and said "Listen, my servant Moses is dead. I'm commissioning you now. I'm appointing you as king of Israel. You have to lead the Israelites out." And God promised him "Wherever your foot should tread will be your land." He continued to encourage him "Do not be discouraged. Do not be dismayed. Don't go to the left, don't go to the right. You stay on that straight and narrow path. Don't be fearful of them, even though they're like thorns and scorpions. Listen, I am with you." That's why later on in the Book of Joshua, Joshua got to a point in his conviction that he told the Israelites when he gathered them, "You have to choose this day whom you will serve. Either the gods—the idolatry of worshiping and serving idols—or you can serve the Great I Am." And then he said "But as for me and my house, we will serve God." It's the evidence of making the right choice and depending on God for the result that will get victory for you every time.

The Green Light Principle

I remember when my sons were smaller. Most of the time, we didn't have any extra money. They would always have their needs met. But if they would ask for something—and it was just something they wanted, not anything they needed—I would share with them, "I don't have a green light with that." I was really saying, "I don't have peace with that right now." And even when I could afford to do what they were asking me to, if I still didn't get a green light, I didn't do it. Later on in life, as they grew up to be men they said "Well dad you just told us 'no' because you didn't want us to have it." But now I'm beginning to see a reflection when I see my oldest son deal with his own kids. He's using that green light principle. Because the reality of it is, if God does not give you peace about something, then you ought not do it. If you find peace with it and you have the peace that comes from the Lord, then that would pretty much be the thing you need to be doing. Now, watch this: just because you have peace about doing something doesn't mean that it's going to be easy.

Your choices with God will always come with consequences that the world will throw at you. And if you're not secure with yourself and your own leadership, you'll begin to bow down to something that's called pride, arrogance, and ego. And you'll become a man-pleaser instead of a God-pleaser. Don't underestimate your choices. Every decision you make have consequences. And there are some choices you make that you won't be able to undo in a lifetime.

Decide Your Convictions Before You Face The Choice

Daniel who was taken out of Jerusalem and into Babylon was confronted by a tremendous challenge to his own faith. "Then the king ordered Ashpenaz, chief of his court officials, to bring in some of the Israelites from the royal family and the nobility, young men without any physical defect, handsome, showing aptitude for every kind of learning, well informed, quick to understand, and qualified to serve in the king's palace. He was to teach them the language and literature of the Babylonians (DANIEL 1:3-4)." He was told that he would be served from the king's table, drinking the king's wine, and eating the king's food, so he could be groomed to serve in Nebachanezzar's court. "But Daniel resolved not to defile himself with the royal food and wine, and he asked the chief official for permission not to defile himself this way (DANIEL 1:8)." Daniel's convictions were in place before he arrived in Babylon. He knew the king's food had probably been offered to idols before arriving on his plate, and that much of it would violate his standards as an Orthodox Jew. He purposed in his heart. He made a decision in his heart before the choice had to be made. If we don't know what we believe about drugs, alcohol, and sexual purity before we are challenged by them, the chances are good that we will fail in that moment of truth.

Christian parents are often much too naïve about what they allow their children to participate in. "My kids are Christians; they wouldn't do that." "This is a Christian group they're going out with. They'll be okay." Young people need to be taught by their parents that, at first indication of questionable activity, they should call a halt to their participation. When the conversation turns to whispers, or bedroom doors are closed, or the truth is shaded, beware something is being planned that is risky.

Be Willing to Die for What You Believe

Think about the other big choice Daniel made. In that day people were supposed to bow down to no other person but the king. But Daniel refused to bow down to the king, and he prayed three or four times a day looking towards Jerusalem. Also Daniel would not eat the food that they were eating. He was sticking to the diet that he had been taught. Because he obeyed God's Law, his enemies came in and said to the king, "Daniel is bowing down to a god other than you." Well, they got the king to sign a decree saying that anybody bowing down to anyone else but the king should be put to death.

Because Daniel refused to bow down to the king of that day, he was cast into the lion's den. We know the story quite well. The king was perplexed because Daniel wasn't fighting or debating about the punishment. Daniel was at the point that he really believed and knew that God was with him. But when they put him in the lion's den, the king, of course, thought the worst would happen to Daniel. But lo and behold, early in the morning when they went to the den, he saw the lion's in the pen but Daniel was still alive. Even more remarkably, because of Daniel's faithfulness, the king committed himself to God and he actually wrote a petition that everybody start serving and worshiping Daniel's God. Also, the result of Daniel's choice to obey God ended up condemning those who plotted against him. The king summoned Daniel's enemies to the lion's den and they were consumed. Ultimately, the impact of Daniel's decision blazed the trail to save a nation of people. Despite peer pressure to compromise what he believed in his heart, Daniel was willing to lay his life down for what he believed to be true. That's why bowing down to God will always deliver you from anything man may try to do against you.

Don't Box with God

Because of Daniel's choice, the king ended up getting saved and converting his country to the God that we know. But had Daniel not made the choice, would that whole area not have been saved? Let's look at what happens if you do not obey God's will. Jonah would be a good example of that.

God was concerned about the people of Nenavah, but Jonah found himself disobeying God. Jonah, in his spirit, could care less about them because they were wicked in their own way. So he pre-judged them. He actually decided to "play god" in their lives. He decided that God can just go ahead and destroy Nenevah because Jonah did not care for the Nenevites at all. And to some degree, it's very tempting for us to play god with people that have rubbed us wrong, people who have either talked about us or insulted or slandered us. We say "God kill them. Get them out of here. They're not worthy of what you've given to me." And yet in our own spirit, we know better, but in some way it makes us feel good when God kills them or destroys them.

But God had a plan for the Nenevites' salvation and he wanted to use Jonah as an instrument to make it happen. Long story short, Jonah got on a boat going the opposite direction from where God sent him. While on the sea, storms came in, rocking the ship back and forth. The captain found Jonah hiding as a stowaway on the ship. And Jonah said "I know why it's storming. I know why we're in this mess. I'm running from God. I'm disobeying God." He said, "The best thing to do to save yourselves, you guys have to throw me over board." Well, at first the captain didn't want that on his hands. And he said "No, we can't do this." Jonah said, "Unless you do this, you will all perish." Jonah was in the air by that time. They threw him off the ship. And just so happens as he was being tossed over, a fish came in and consumed him and swallowed him whole. He's still alive inside of this particular whale or fish.

The crazy thing is, I see a lot of leaders who find themselves going into lock-down. Sometimes it's corporal punishment and corrections, jail, and those kind of things. But even you can have a jail within your own mind or in your own life, where you actually put your own self in jail. And so now what happens? Jonah is in there not for one day, not for two days, but for three days. It's as if God said, "I wanna keep you in the dark long enough until you realize, your arms are way too short to box with me. My Will-will ultimately come to be, because everything that I decide will come to fruition. And if I'm gonna use you and I've chosen you, I'm gonna use you." And so when the fish spewed him out on dry land Jonah got busy. He headed to Nenevah.

Isn't it kind of sad that you might make the wrong choices knowing you still have to do the work. It's like when we were home as kids. Mother says, "Listen, tonight is your night to wash these dishes. Make sure you clean them really well. Make sure you put them all up. And you gotta mop this floor. And you gotta make sure everything is done and everything is tidy before you go to bed."

You say, "Well yes ma'am. That's what I'm gonna do. Thank you, mamma. Goodnight. Love you." But, your little, lazy self sits there and watches some more TV. You watch a re-run of Soul Train. And by the time Soul Train finishes, another movie comes on. Now, it's one o'clock in the morning. And it dawns on you that you haven't actually washed the dishes. You haven't cleaned the kitchen or anything. And so you go in there half-heartedly trying to move some stuff around. You're tired; you're fatigued. You gave your energy to things you wanted to do rather than what your parent wanted you to do. So here you are. You go to bed to sleep.

Mamma gets up about four in the morning, goes in the kitchen, and realizes you didn't do anything. You didn't even wipe off the stove. So now it's five o'clock and you're wondering why you're getting straps on your head, waking you out of a deep sleep. That's a terrible feeling! Now you have get up. You're crying. You haven't even brushed your teeth. Your breath stinks. You're miserable. You're tired, and now, you have to go wash those dishes, while you're crying and full of tears. And then you have to hear your mamma scolding you while you're doing it. Your siblings are in the room laughing at you. Talking about, "Thank God it ain't me." "I told him." "I told her." So the key is, it's always wiser to make sure, you don't underestimate your choices. Follow the simple rule of thumb: Obedience to God is recommended over sacrifices. Follow the Spirit. The Spirit will never lead you wrong.

Life Letter

Pastor August has been such a great example of a leader, not only at Church but also in the community. Pastor August is so mission minded. He does not only talk about the right thing to do but does it as well "Not just a hearer of the word, but a doer as well. Pastor is really a man after God's own heart, has such a compassion for his people, is always prayerful and observant of his surroundings—a "WATCHMAN ON THE WALL." Pastor is very committed to being a servant of the Most High God. It is not about Pastor Walter August, but about God with his favorite scripture, GALATIANS 2:20, "Being crucified with Christ."

Whatever is going on at the Church and Bethel's Family you can count on Pastor August being hands on. If it is setting up chairs emptying trash or whatever needs doing, because of the example and sincerity he presents to the body, the other men are willing to serve as well. If pastor is aware of any ungodly situations he is quick to give godly counsel and correction.

He is not only concerned about the children, but the seniors as well, and instructs us to continue on from whatever age we are. You are still useful in the kingdom!

Pastor is always about excellence and getting things done. When there is something to be done Pastor does not give up easily. He is serious and committed, though there are times he will break the ice with humor.

I thank God that Pastor is serious about the mission God has him on and for being under the leadership of a man of order.

BETTY PEACOCK, CHURCH RECEPTIONIST

CHAPTER FIVE

Speak and Think Like a Leader

"Do not let any unwholesome talk come out of your mouths, but only what is helpful for building others up according to their needs, that it may benefit those who listen (Ephesians 4:29)."

THIS IS THE Bible's version of "If you can't say something nice, don't say anything at all." We ought to speak only words that build up and encourage others. "This does not mean that you negate issues of sin in people's live (II Samuel 2, Nathan to King David; Matthew 18:15). This one passage, if consistently obeyed would eliminate the overwhelming majority of life's conflicts. Words of a mature Christian seek to help the listeners, not harm them.

Leaders, Watch Your Mouths

The tongue is a small organ, but it can control and influence major events in your life. James, the half-brother of Jesus show us the power of the tongue. In the Bible, James states:

> When we put bits into the mouth of horses to make them obey us, we can turn the whole animal. Or take ships as an example. Although they are so large and are driven by strong winds, they are steered by a very small rudder wherever the pilot wants to go. Likewise the tongue is a small part of the body, but it makes great boasts. Consider what a great forest is set on fire by a small spark. The tongue also is a fire, a world of evil among the parts of the body. It corrupts the whole person, sets the whole course of his life on fire, and is itself set on fire by hell (JAMES 3:3-6).

By nature the tongue could serve as a divisive instrument of evil. By grace the tongue can become an instrument of positive blessings (COL.4:6). We must not conclude the tongue is doomed to be an instrument of discord and strife. God can mold an abusive tongue into a force for good and righteousness. The tongue can produce ruin and may represent the presence of a vast system of iniquity within our body. Within this body the tongue can produce three results: First, it can corrupt the whole person, it is a source of pollution and defilement for the entire personality. Secondly, it sets the whole course of life on fire. A misused tongue may affect the cycle of life from birth onward! Thirdly, the tongue is itself set on fire by hell. This describes Satan's influence on the tongue.

In the book of Isaiah, God's people continued their moaning and their accusing God of inactivity on their behalf. Isaiah was confident because he had found his God-given mission. "The Sovereign LORD has given me an instructed tongue, to know the word that sustains the weary. He wakens me morning by morning, wakens my ear to listen like one being taught (ISAIAH 50:4)." He had a word of comfort because he listened to God for a new word every day, every morning. Isaiah was surrounded by a bunch of complainers and in the mist of this negativity, he knew the only thing that kept him from using his mouth for foolishness was his communion with God.

Leaders, Always Communicate With Wisdom

All believers in the Lord Jesus Christ must speak with wisdom from God. "Let your conversation be always full of grace seasoned with salt, so that you may know how to answer everyone (COLOSSIANS 4:6)." Our communication is to be gracious, charming, and always seasoned with salt. Salt was used for two purposes in Paul's time. It was used as a preservative to keep food from spoiling. This means that believers talk is to be free from corruption, wholesome. Salt was also used as an additive to give flavor to food. Our talk must be interesting, witty, tactful, and appealing.

In Acts, chapter five, Peter and John were chastised and arrested for teaching and preaching in Jesus's name, after being ordered not to do so. When they were brought before the Sanhedrin (the whole high council of the Israelites) and they were accused of teaching in Jesus's name. Peter went on a rampage against the Jewish leadership, letting them know that they had crucified Jesus Christ, an innocent man. And conviction fell on them, so they wanted to kill Peter and John. But Gamaliel, a teacher of the law and a great leader of the people, had Peter and John put outside while he spoke to the assembly. He said, "you have to be careful with these men, because other men have come before them, claiming that they have some newfound wisdom. But we left them alone and each one of those individuals came to nothing." He said, "Let these men go because if it's not of God, you don't have to worry about anything." But then he says, "I must warn you, if it is of God, then you'll be fighting, not against these men, but against God. And we are not prepared to fight against God." That wisdom was embraced. They brought Peter and John back in, flogged them, and set them free. Peter left, filled with joy that he could identify with the suffering of Christ for the cause of the gospel. These are examples of men following Christ, no matter what. When you're on the hot seat, you have to still be a Christian. As a matter of fact, you must be Christian to the core. Every layer of you, when people start peeling your life back, it should still show Christ, even to your enemies.

Leaders, Expand Your Horizon

Leaders must read. A leader has to spend more time reading than they do talking. So when you *do* open up your mouth, you've got something of quality and content to say. And you're not just putting a lot of hot air out there with no substance, and so a leader has to be reading, got to be knowledgeable.

Another crucial thing I often share with leaders is this: it's important for you to read the newspapers. Don't just read the sports section. As leaders, especially from humble beginnings, you need to read the entire newspaper. That's why they printed everything. You don't go in there and buy one section of newspaper. They give you a whole one. Now, what you discard is up to you. I discard the sales paper, because I am not a shopper. If you see me in the mall, somebody's in serious trouble. If you see me at the mall, I'm sitting down, waiting on someone to come find me.

But the reality with newspapers is that you should read from cover to cover. You look at State; you look at World; you look at local news and you cover the gamut. If you wake up in the morning and you read the newspaper, I guarantee you, when you go into any room, anywhere, at any time of the day, you can hold an intelligent conversation with anybody on a variety of things because you have actually spurred on your intellect. And you have to always have a thirst for more knowledge.

You have to expand your horizon, so when you go into a room — no matter who's in that room, no matter the socioeconomic status, no matter what the situation is for that particular group of people — you can communicate with them at a level that is palatable, for an understanding and an intelligent conversation to take place that impacts their lives, regardless of what level they are on.

Leaders, Know Your Audience

One of the things that is crucial in the area of communicating, number one: you have to know your audience. Think about commercials that you see on television. Normally, the audience level for the commercial industry is that of a typical fifth grader, a ten or eleven year old kid. It's important that they speak to that level because they don't want to spend millions of dollars on airtime for a commercial that doesn't register with the common viewer. They want to make sure when the audience watches the commercial, kids are begging their parents to go get a new iPad. You have to know your audience.

Also, be mindful that you don't lord your intellect over one that might not have that depth of knowledge or academic success. We see it so often. For example, when we go to Kenya, we think we're smart and have all this intelligence. We speak what we call "correct English," but they *really* speak correct English because the British colonized Kenya. So they speak English better than we do in America. Here is the issue: in our mind-frame, being Americans, we are indoctrinated to think that we're smarter than everybody. And so when we go places, we look at their language, it might be a little bit different, the dialect might be a little different and somehow it is kind of funny that they talk differently. You can go to my own hometown in Louisiana. My parents speak broken French. And so you have to pay careful attention to some of the things they're saying. Even with me, sometimes, I don't put all the syllables in place. Sometimes if I'm writing, the punctuation, the periods, the right words might not be in place, because I write how I speak, and based on those mind-frames you have to be knowledgeable enough to know when and how to communicate without degrading, without discouraging, without insulting. So when you speak, even from somebody that's in poverty, you want to speak from a level where you can connect with them. As leaders, that is something in which we have to do a better job.

Leaders, Communicate with wisdom

You have to spend a lot of time with God. You have to really spend a lot of time with God. Some wisdom is what we call wisdom that comes from just natural learning, but the greater wisdom comes from the Word of God. It comes from—sometimes God gives you things that you can't otherwise get, only when you ask him to give it to you. The Book of James, chapter one, it says "If any of you lack wisdom, why don't you go and ask God, who gives wisdom liberally, without finding fault?" In order to get this wisdom, you must seek it out from the Lord. And then wisdom, I often share the difference between knowledge and wisdom. There are people that can know the truth in their mind-framing brains, and they know, if I go into this store and pull that can of beer off that shelf and run out of the store, the police is coming, and there is a probability that I am going to be arrested. Now, I know that to be true. If I go into a bank with a gun and go up to the teller and tell her, "It's a stick-up." I know it's a federal offense. And when they catch me—not if but when they catch me, I will be going to federal prison. I know that quite well. Right now, if I took this bare hand and slapped your face real hard. Your glasses will fly over there. You will holler and your dad comes running in here. "What's going on?" Your dad and I are going to be fighting all in here. I know that. That is knowledge. But even though, knowing what is going to happen, people still do it. Wisdom must come in. Well, you say, "Now that you know what can happen, is that what you really want to happen?" So you start thinking Rodney King. You start thinking Chad Holley. You start thinking about things before you actually execute it. Wisdom will give you the results before you even begin to open the door. And so you make your decision: To sleep or not to sleep. That is the question.

Life Letters

There is not a day that goes by that I do not thank God for Pastor August speaking the words in my life. I have been receiving the bread of life through Pastor August, who will always be my spiritual leader. That is what a leader does and that is speak to the souls of men, women, and children to ignite a spiritual flame so that I can go and proclaim the goodness of God and allow God to get the glory for my life.

Pastor August's wisdom is prevalent in him as a leader. Pastor August exemplifies the excellent attributes of an effective spiritual leader. When I listen to his vision and I know he is walking in faith to God, I see the prayers of a righteous man revealed.

Ms. Dorothy Henson

Pastor August is a living testimony of the phrase, "In order to be a good leader one must first learn to be a good follower." He has shown me that as a leader of God's people one must be willing to exercise faith, especially in things you know God is calling you to do. Under his leadership I've learned that a leader is a person who guides others towards a goal or inspires them to believe. Pastor August has demonstrated that a leader possesses qualities such as confidence, persuasion, and motivation.

One thing that has ministered to me the most about his leadership is the non-negotiable act of loving the Lord our God with all our heart, mind, and soul; loving our neighbors as we love ourselves; and loving our wives and children unconditionally.

Mr. Jeff Campbell,
Trinity Investment Properties, LLC

CHAPTER SIX

Visionary Impact

Visionary Leadership

GOD LOOKS FOR men and women, who are biblically committed to cast vision, set goals, mobilize the Body of Christ, and overcome obstacles in order to reach the nations for Christ. Do you have to be a visionary to be a leader? Do you have to have a vision for the future in order to be a leader?

Every person ought to have a vision, even if it is only about where *you* are going. Because without a vision, scripture says, people perish. And so, as a leader without a vision, you're just taking a walk. Thom S. Rainer speaks about the leaders that God uses. And he lists six qualifications in his book, "Breakout Churches: Discover How to Make the Leap." One, top tier qualifications, is that he is a God-called leader. Secondly, he is passionate about what God has called for him to do. Thirdly, he is a contributing leader. He doesn't just talk; he writes his checks. Because if you don't actually invest in what you say you've been called to do, there is a high probability you haven't been called to do it. Fourthly, he's an outwardly thinking, outwardly focused leader. Yes, we're the church. If you're already saved, that's wonderful. But I can't just continually look at you, all the time. We have to begin to look outside the church. There are some kids out there who are not in church.

Leadership In the Community

In 1994 there was an apartment complex called The Huntington Place Apartments in Southwest Houston. Right now, it is currently Bayou Village Apartments. But back in '94, crime was at an all-time high at this apartment. Anything you wanted that the devil was selling or giving away, you could get it. There was so much crime on the property that when police officers received a call, they would wait across the street at the store until at least three or four car units showed up before they came in. It was a place called "hell" all by itself. That's the place that God called us to go start a church — in hell.

Two years after my call in the ministry, I had no seminary training. I just believed God's Word. My wife and our little family, we weren't smart enough to figure out we were not equipped to go in there. But we went out of the obedience of the call of God over our lives. So, we went in to the apartments. I talked to the managers and owners. Because of the crime and liability that they were going up against, they were willing to try anything. So why not try Jesus? They gave us three apartment unit (with two bedrooms and two baths) plus the clubhouse — exclusively — to use as we may. Long story short, within six months we took the clubhouse and we made it our little worship/Bible study area/fellowship hall—that's what we needed. One apartment became our Sunday School area and classroom for the kids; another apartment, we made our soup kitchen, our cafeteria where we gave families supper and breakfast on Saturdays for the kids. In another apartment, I moved a couple on-site to act as our directors, so we always had eyes and ears on the property.

We started the church with eleven people, five to seven of them were my family members. The property owners were going to see what would happen. And within six months we outgrew the clubhouse. We moved to the nearby school and continued to work through the apartments. But what was happening? Children were getting hope. A lot of these kids in the community today, I baptized in the swimming pool at the apartments and now they're educated. They're married with their own families. We're still in the same community that we've been ministering in, and the community has stabilized because we are here. That whole apartment complex has been cleaned of the drugs and harmful elements. People were wanting to come in. The elements were going out. Because whenever the light comes in, darkness has to get out. And even in the community that we're in, I still say it's a "soul mine." This community is better because we're here. Our facilities, the ministries that we offer, it brings about community stabilization.

We built a double gymnasium for recreation. And we have non-profits to minister to entire populations. Whether its business, education, or dealing with the economy and getting people's money right, those things we put out there because it is right. And then when it comes down to spiritual development and nourishment, we have a five-fold ministry that opens and runs with all barrels loaded. We are operating every day. There is something going on within what Bethel's Family is doing. So every single day somebody's doing something on this campus because our motto is, and desire has always been, to be a church that never closes. So right here in the Fondren, Southwest Community, even the property and what has been built here, the Lord has definitely lead us here. It speaks volumes of excellence. It speaks volumes that someone cares. In the midst of a crazy community, there are bright spots. And when you mention the church or when you mention Bethel's Family, it speaks about how we take care of you with food; we take care of you educationally; the Pastor has a good name, there's some integrity to the Ministry, and so I want to be a part of that. And that is why 90% of all of our leaders and core givers don't live in this community. People are driving from around the city to come here—around the cities: Katy, Humble, and La Porte. They are coming here because we do missions. We have a mission field. It is not to see what color suit the Pastor has on and how he's going to preach, whoop, and shout. It is because we are actually impacting the community.

Leaders Affecting International Communities

Life spins out based on what the others are doing around you, especially as children. That's why I continue to have a strong passion for our youth. I advocate going to Africa, doing what we're doing for those who are without, because I identify. I can affiliate with them; I can understand people coming by, bringing clothing and food to your house. I understand all of that quite well, so it's easy for me to have compassion—not just sympathy, but true compassion. Enough to where I want to do something to make it better. Also, it gives us a greater appreciation for the power of God, allowing his scriptures to fulfill themselves in and through your life, out of an obedient walk with him.

Take, for instance, our mission's pastor, Marcus Holman. Pastor Holman is a banker, but he also has a strong love for the Lord. He started Bethel's Global Reach and lead our largest mission team of people, at one time—93 people on one trip, to do medical, dental, evangelistic and other work. We went to Kenya in Africa; set up a medical clinic; saw thousands of people; brought professional dentists and doctors and nurses; and then we left those places. The last place we visited was in Miguta, Kenya, and we left the pharmacy fully stocked. The pastor of a church there hired a doctor to come in to continue the work. So the dentists, the doctors examining, the medication are still there. They are handing them out. We will continue to partner with and make shipments to them. We have some dental chairs in storage to ship to them, so that they can have a fully set-up clinic. Because we can get medicine here pretty easily, so we, from time to time, do shipments. And every year when we do missions, we can send a medical team to their location to encourage them in what they're doing. So lives are being changed.

The other thing, when it comes down to the Gospel Message, people get to feel Jesus by *the work* that we do. The words that we say are always measured by what we do — especially when we go abroad. So internationally, the medical global reach, Marcus Holman, what it's doing for him and his family, drawing new people who have never been on a mission trip, taking young people on a mission trip for the first time, and giving them a real missionary experience — they know their hands have been used by God to be a blessing in somebody else's life. One of the ministry opportunities that we have, we call it the Foot Washing Ministry because many of the families, and especially in Kenya in the rural areas, they have a foot bacteria called "jiggers." And they are little fleas that get into the cracks of the heel because a lot of people walk with no shoes on. But jiggers are flesh-eating. So if you can imagine the crust of your foot continually being eaten away over a series of years and the damage the bacteria are having on your foot. Feet are very vital to your mobility. So the Foot Washing Ministry goes and they wash feet.

When we went to Miguta, they set up four washing stations. These lines never got short the three days we were there. They washed feet from the time we arrived, to the time we got ready to leave. And the next morning, the lines were already waiting for us. It is unbelievable, when you look at the impact. I got an email from that pastor. It's awesome. What God is doing through Marcus Holman and Bethel's Global Reach is phenomenal.

Life Letters

Pastor Walter August is a man of vision. I have had the privilege of serving under his leadership for almost seven years and during this time I have witnessed how God has used him to affect his local community and places abroad. In my opinion, there are three components to Pastor August that have contributed to his success in ministry and helped shaped the ministry God has given me: His devotion to his family, his servant leadership, and his strength as a visionary.

Pastor August often quips, "One of the hardest things a person can do, is plant a church." As a new church planter, I am finding this statement to be very true. However, I have the privilege of being planted from a church (Bethel's Family) and a pastor that values church planting and growth. This is not just a verbal support, but he has personally poured heavily into the new ministry and avails himself to me in times of need.

I am thankful to have a pastor who trusts God with all that he has. He is not only my Pastor, but like a father to me. I am thankful for his vision and leadership.

Pastor Lawrence Scott

Pastor August is a great man, pastor, and role model. I honestly don't know any other pastors who truly care about people all over the world. He is truly a giver giving all that he can to everyone that needs help here locally and completing missions saving people lives internationally. We are thankful for Pastor August and pray for him and our church's mission daily.

Thank You for your hard work and executing what God has given and is still giving you.

ASHLEY LEE

My family and I have had the good fortune of being a part of his ministry work since 2002. During such time, I have experienced countless opportunities doing God's work under Pastor August's stewardship, whereby I benefited from his steadfast leadership and God-centered views of life and life lessons.

With that being said, I see Pastor August as a servant's servant, which makes him an extremely successful leader among leaders. Yet, the most significant aspect of Pastor August's leadership attributes is that he is a visionary leader truly after God's heart. His visionary impact spans across the globe from the Czech Republic to Africa to Haiti to South America to the depressed areas of North America. Pastor August is an "Actions Speak Louder than Words" missionary leader who takes to heart the Great Commission.

As a local community leader, Pastor August has solidly established the Bethel's brand—Bethel meaning "House of God." Out of God's church that Pastor August shepherds, he has birthed numerous community service organizations such as Bethel's Heavenly Hands (food pantry and thrift store), Bethel's Place (community and family services), Bethel's Global Reach (domestic and international missions), Bethel's Community Development Center (all services facility), Bethel's PLACE Property & Management (Community Revitalization, Housing and Real Estate), Bethel's iCare Social Services (connecting social services to match community needs), Bethel's Christian Academy (Christian based—toddlers to pre-school education), and Bethel's Place Vocational & Technology College (offering vocational and technical training certification).

May the good Lord continue to bless and keep Pastor August as he continues to put God first in his life, and shepherd God's people in working to continue His kingdom-building here on earth as it is in heaven.

MR. LEON JENKINS, LIEUTENANT COLONEL,
U.S. ARMY RETIRED, BUSINESS OWNER

I didn't grow up with a father who taught me the Word of God or challenged me to be better than standard. There was no vision cast for my future. The Bible says in Proverbs 29:18, "Where there is no vision the people are unrestrained."

A visionary is a person with unusual foresight and faith in someone who constantly sees the impossible as possible with God. He's not an illusionist. He sincerely trusts God to do the things he cannot, while every time doing what he can.

MS. PRICILLA BOOKER

I have known Walter August for over a decade. He has always been a man of vision, a man who could see beyond the present, a man who walks by faith and not by sight. There has never been a time talking with him where he has been satisfied with what existed. It seemed that vision was in his DNA. Once I heard Robert Schuler say: "The greatest church has not been built." Schuler said this at a time when he led a ministry to be envied by the overwhelming majority of pastors in America. This same perspective emanates from Walter. The greatest has not yet come! It hasn't happened! It is yet to be developed! No matter what he has accomplished, he constantly peers into the future of possibilities of what could be improved, purchased, built, corrected, torn down, developed, and so on. This has had quite an impact on my life.

Walter's visionary make-up is contagious. There was a season in my life and ministry when I could not see beyond my predicament. I saw myself as a failure. God used him to encourage me to focus on the possibilities of the future and not the pain of the past.

While some leaders only get excited about their vision, what God has revealed to them and is doing through them, Walter gets excited persuading others about their own possibilities. This is rare. I have learned from him to follow what the Word of says: "Write the vision; make it plain...so he may run who reads it (Habakkuk 2:2)." Walter is not just a dreamer; he is an organized administrative visionary. He reduces to writing what God reveals to him. There are principles to abide by and processes to follow.

The leaders and members under his leadership are equipped to run with the vision. They have taken ownership of it, knowing the vision is not for him alone, it is for them and the community they serve. Those who make up Bethel's Family live and breathe its vision.

One can see what was seen by the visionary. One can touch what he talked about. One can now hear what he heard in the spirit. I thank God for Walter and the visionary impact he's had on his community, our city, and my life.

Pastor John D. Ogletree, Jr.,
First Metropolitan Church, Houston, Texas

CHAPTER SEVEN

True Friends and Prayer

Accountability of Leaders

WHY IS ACCOUNTABILITY important for the leader? There are areas that we need to be mindful of as leaders, and I teach this to my staff. When I was on staff with Sugar Creek Baptist Church, Dr. Mark Hartman, the Senior Pastor, also taught this to our staff. He was dealing with the subject of moral integrity as leaders.

There are three areas that are traps for every leader. One is fatigue. Fatigue happens when you have so much as a leader. You have so many people competing for your time that your phone is blowing up, and your email box is full. If you are texting, if you're trying to keep up with all your tweets, and your texts, all that can play a part. You've got family; you've got kids; you've got sons; you've got grandkids; you've got appointments; you've got meetings. You've got building meetings; you've got deacon's meetings; you've got trustee meetings. You have to prepare messages. Your time is limited. Fatigue sets in. And before you know it, you don't know Monday from Sunday. And just like you don't know Monday from Sunday, you don't know your wife from your secretary. Follow me? That's fatigue.

The second thing is flattery. "Pastor, you're the best pastor in the whole world. I ain't never heard nobody preach like that." Your head gets big. Your ego gets inflated. "Pastor, you've got it going on. I heard you're a visionary pastor!" If you believe everything people write about you or say about you, that puffs you up. Your head gets so big you can't even leave the church. Your head can't fit through the doors. Flattery will mess you up as a leader.

The third one is an oxymoron: Your own success can become your greatest failure. Every leader wants to get to a point in his or her life where they can look back and say, "How do you like me now?" Your success can become you greatest failure, because we live in a success-driven world. You are known, not by your content of character or your moral stance on the issues, but you are known by your bank account. So you can be a very fraudulent brother, a wicked brother, but if your bank is strong, you can get invited to all the parties. We can get puffed up with success, thinking we've done something on our own. But we have only done what God has allowed us to do. And so we have to always remember: if it had not been for God, we could not have done anything. Without God, it's impossible to see the miracles that only God can do, but man often takes credit for what God has done. Fatigue, flattery, and the failure of success: as leaders, you've got to be on guard against all three.

Living a Life of Accountability

Well, you have to live within the symmetry of what God put around you. I thank God, in his infinite wisdom, that he places the right people around you, but you have to have a heart to welcome that accountability. Because even though leaders have people around them all the time, they may not welcome being challenged in their accountability to God. Flesh doesn't want to be checked or challenged by anybody. Believe it or not, if I am walking foul and you come to me, and say, "Listen, pastor, I'm not sure if you're picking this up about this decision that you made and why you made it, but it seems like it contradicts what God said you should be doing." Well, like that Michael Jackson song, my spirit ought to be to first to look at the man in the mirror. When you respond and say, "Who are you?" you are not seeking the righteousness of God. I only have a 180 degree view, and I might not see what's happening behind me. You might be seeing what I haven't seen, because sometimes we're the last ones to see our own failures. You've got to find a way to embrace constructive criticism as a leader. If leaders don't do that, then they turn more dictatorial. And that begins to cause real rifts within the body of Christ.

So, it's good to have the people that God has put around you. And allow them to have some level of say-so. If they see something, they need to go ahead and help you because it is not a matter to destroy you. If I check you on something, I want to make you better. I don't want you to fail. For the most part, we fail greatly because we see stuff happening and we don't say anything about it. Look at Joe Paterno, a Penn State coaching legend.

He and others knew about assistant coach Jerry Sandusky's alleged sexual abuse of young boys but did not actually do anything about it. And so Paterno's career is tarnished by associating with this element but not reporting it.

In the Book of Ezekiel, chapters two and three, Ezekiel explained his call from God to lead and to do what God has asked him to do. And God tells him, "Listen, when I tell you to go tell a man about what he's doing that's wrong and you refuse to go tell him, his blood will also be on your hands because you refused to go tell him what I told you." If I see you doing wrong and I don't correct you, then your sin falls on me too, as a believer. But we live in a world where leaders don't confront other leaders directly. And we have to be more bold in that area. It is not going to make us popular. I can tell you that. But God has never called for us to be popular. He called for us to live the way His Word says that we should. Even Jesus chastens the ones he loves.

Human Arrogance versus Accountability

In Psalm 10, God's apparent absence made the wicked bold. The wicked one "says to himself, 'God has forgotten; he covers his face and never sees' (PSALMS 10:11)." In this Psalm, they were not atheists but secular Jews. They said, "There is no God, I shall not meet adversity." So these people proceeded to prey on the poor, fearing no punishment. They said, "God has forgotten he will never see. God will never call us to account." Therefore, they thought they were immune from divine judgment. Showing that human arrogance knows no limits.

In the Old Testament text, David was a king that had everything from God: palaces, kingdoms, armies. He enjoyed an intimate walk with God, a family, a stable political position, and an unbroken string of military victories. The only thing that King David did not have was another man's wife. So David saw this woman, Bathsheba, bathing one day who was married to a man named Uriah. David thought he had no one to answer to and so he committed adultery and murder recorded in 2nd Samuel. Apparently, nobody dared to question this poor and sad decision.

Even after God blessed him calling him "a man after God's own heart," King David, when he slept with Bathsheba, was approached by a prophet. The prophet gave him just a story that God had put in his spirit. He said there was a man who had a little lamb—only one lamb. That was all he had. He loved the lamb so much and the lamb would sleep in the bed with the family. They had a neighbor across the street. The neighbor had this great, big farm with many animals, the whole nine yards—had it going on. This neighbor had a visitor come by one evening. Instead of the actual neighbor going into his own yard, stocking and pulling a lamb or goat and preparing it for the visitor who came to visit *him*, he went across the street to this man who only had one lamb and took that man's lamb.

Well, when he told that story, it infuriated David. David said, "What did he do? Took that—what? Well, give me his name. I'm going to make him pay four times as much." And the prophet said, "David, you are that man."

David said four times as much. If you think about it, not only did the son that he and Bathsheba conceived die, but also one other son raped his own sister. Two victims automatically — a rapist and now a victim of rape. The older son, Absalom, David's oldest son, killed his brother, Ammon, because he raped his sister. Now David has a son who is a murderer, two dead sons, and a raped daughter. That's four children. So when you think about leadership we have to continue to allow people to speak into our lives, allow some level of transparency. And I don't mean "put your stuff on the flagpole," but I think if you teach and preach transparency, it will draw the kind of people you want around you. And that way, you can always be yourself.

It is hard to do, though. But at the end of the day, you gotta face your family. You have to face your children and what's important to you. What is important to you? If the Word of God is not important to you, what can I say. Effective people hold themselves accountable just like everyone else they know. Maintaining such accountability involves seeking complete honesty. Effective people consistently receive feedback from those who work with them. People who fail to provide a structure for accountability will lead to a crisis of character and leadership. Again, you've got to leave this place better than you found it.

A Leader Needs True Friends

It is good to have friends — not many. You don't need a whole bucket of friends. This is not Facebook. I do believe you have to have people who you can put into your intimate circle. Christ definitely demonstrated that with his close relationship to Peter,

James, and John. He loved all of his disciples, but when he did certain things, he would take Peter, James, and John. When he went up to the Mountain of Transfiguration, Peter, James, and John got the invitation to that. When it came down to him in the Garden of Gethsemane for his time of prayer, he brought his disciples in, took some to a certain length, went a little further in, took a few more. He had an inner circle.

Every man, every person, every leader needs to have an inner circle of intercessors for prayer. It allows you to know you're being covered with somebody who knows how to pray. There are times, in our flesh, that our bodies get tired. We get weak. We already know we are terminal. We are strong in many different areas, but we also know this life does have an expiration date. It is a terrible thing to be a leader and have no true friends. As a matter of fact, that's not a good position for anyone. Remember, King David's moral failings? His tragedy underscores what can happen when people fail to create a structure in which they are answerable for how they spend their private and professional time. While David could hide his sins from associates, he couldn't hide them from God. God sent the prophet, Nathan, to confront King David. The king discovered that even kings are accountable for their actions. Effective people don't wait for crisis to establish accountability. Do you have someone to whom you are accountable for in your private and professional life?

Is a friend loving at all times? Friends should not be defined by the world. Friends should be defined based on what God has said a friend is. A friend sees the best in you when others only see the worst in you. Friends are there, through thick and thin. A friendship has no boundaries — real friendship. Friendship will get into you and agitate you. Even though you don't want to hear the truth, they'll still say it. Friends will jeopardize the relationship to maintain the integrity of the truth that is in God. So by all means, the resource of friends proves invaluable to a leader. To *not* have friends as a resource is destructive.

Prayer is Key

Babies have a natural instinct when discerning who is good and who is bad. They really do. Pay attention to children when they cry. You try to pass them off to somebody, but the child will cry and tell you, "no." The child senses something that we are not seeing. We're just trying to be polite. But there is a special sense that the child sees, feels, and experiences that we need to consider. That's why when they are very young they need the greatest protection their parents can give.

So when choosing friends, ask God to show you, to lead you, and to lead those individuals *to you* versus you just going out and saying, "You, you, and you. Ya'll come with me." Prayer is the key. I don't trust myself when choosing friends because I've failed many times with people that I thought had my best interest at heart. Every man or woman can do a nice little dog-and-pony show if they know you are watching. But you need to pray. The Holy Spirit will never lead you wrong.

But be careful, if you ever go before the Lord asking him to put specific people in your life that he has not sent to you. Their main job may be to mess you up. They will come in as a friend, propping you up and telling you all the things you want to hear.

At the same time, they have their hand on that rug that you're standing on, and they're just waiting. As soon as they're ready, they pull the rug. And they say, "Gotcha!"

Continue to have a strong spirit of discernment and be willing to listen to that spirit. When you are in tune with God, and you begin to ask God about an individual, when this individual comes around, God is going to have you feel something. Proverbs says, "trust the Lord with all your heart, and do not rely on your own understanding. Acknowledge him in all your ways and he will make your paths straight (3:5-6)." That's true all the time, if you are praying to allow the Lord to show you who you need to have around you.

Prayer is Paramount

Prayer is as the breath we take. The Scriptures say that men ought always pray, every breath I take, it ought to have an essence of some inspiration of prayer to the Lord, even if it is just on the breath saying, "Thank you, God. I need you, God. You are awesome, God." It is a continual flow of dialogue.

Have you ever been in love? When you are in love, it is a natural desire to want to hear that voice, to want to speak to that person, to want to see that person. When you are in love with somebody—when you truly love them—you desire to talk to them all of the time. The greatest love affair there is, is between a Holy God and his precious people. And for the people, there must be a strong desire to always be in the presence of the Lord, and that is through prayer. And prayer is not directly or divinely doing a whole lot of talking. It is always better to listen to what

God says than to keep talking, because many times a teacher will know more than the student. In God's case, He always knows more. Sometimes he speaks only through his Word. And in the Biblical realm, in a spiritual sense, if you want to get the best out of your efforts and your time, listen to what God says. Prayer is paramount. No prayer, no power. No power, no peace. No peace, no joy. No joy, sorrow.

Life Letters

"And not just for some things, but, in all things we trust you God". This is how Pastor Walter August ended most of his prayers. Prayer is something that I have always known growing up in church.

At 40 years old I have never have the opportunity to meet, see, or even speak to my biological father. Having him abandon me at only a few months old, I struggled severely with trusting men in my life—and even more so, the idea of God, who was a "Father." I often said to myself, to justify my contention and my unbelief, that "If my biological father would leave me, how could I ever trust a father who I can't see?" As I reflect on it now, I see that my deep-seated issues of trust had a profound effect on my prayer life, or the lack thereof. I thank God that His plans are not my plans, and my plans are not His plans (Isaiah 55:8), because little did I know, God was going to show me what a trusting Father looked like.

Pastor Walter August has, in so many ways, been the biological father that I never had. Ironically enough, Pastor August had the same testimony of "fatherlessness" as I did. I watched how he did not allow the issues of his past to affect his future, but saw him press on with greater determination. I have learned that trust still is a quality that is to be admired and, even more, expected. Pastor August has shown me the effects of prayer when, in essence, that was all that he had.

Pastor Marcus D. Holman

Pastor August has guided me through some tough times with my family. On several occasions; Pastor August has talked and prayed with me concerning my estranged relationship with my brother.

His concern for people is shown through his actions. He invited me over for dinner one Friday night. I felt special being served dinner by my pastor and the First Lady [of the church]. He allowed me to talk freely about what I wanted to talk about. He doesn't just talk the talk but he walks and talks what he is trying to convey to you. It is through his teaching, time, and prayers that this relationship will be mended and our mother will be happy before she leaves this earth.

He's always been there for me. He returns calls, emails, and answers texts. We are talking about a diverse friendship here.

If you know Pastor August, you have a friend for life. He will keep those prayers going up for you.

Thank you God for sharing Pastor August with us here on earth!

Dr. Schuwan Dorsey,
Professor/Educator Consultant

Pastor August has been a true friend as well as an awesome spiritual leader. The friendship I have developed with Pastor August is truly a gift from God. During my times of sadness, sorrow, and depression, I could call on Pastor August and he would always be there.

When my husband had a serious stroke on the right side, Pastor August made a visit to the hospital to counsel both of us. Four years later, my father had a serious stroke, but didn't make it. Pastor made numerous visits and prayed with my family. Then after that, one of my nephews was murdered. I called Pastor, and he attended and participated in the funeral. Four and half years later, my mother developed gangrene in both feet due to poor circulation. She was given 4 months to live. Pastor came prayed and talked to all of my family members. Pastor August's dedication truly signifies his commitment to The Church at Bethel's Family.

Mrs. Marsha G. Jones-Sylvester,
Retired, U.S. Postal Service

Final Note on Leadership

The ultimate goal of a leader, if we are in the spiritual context—and even if it is a secular context—is to work in such a way that others will see God in you. And they will not only see Him, but they will also feel Him. You've got to keep your face in the presence of God, and they'll feel his presence. The goal of the "bootstrap leader" is to truly live and lead by example. Be the greatest encourager you know how to be. Even toward the person with the minimal level of giftedness, find something to encourage. Be willing to pay the hard price. And that price is "everything."